Dolphins Coloring Book For Adults

This book belongs to:

_____

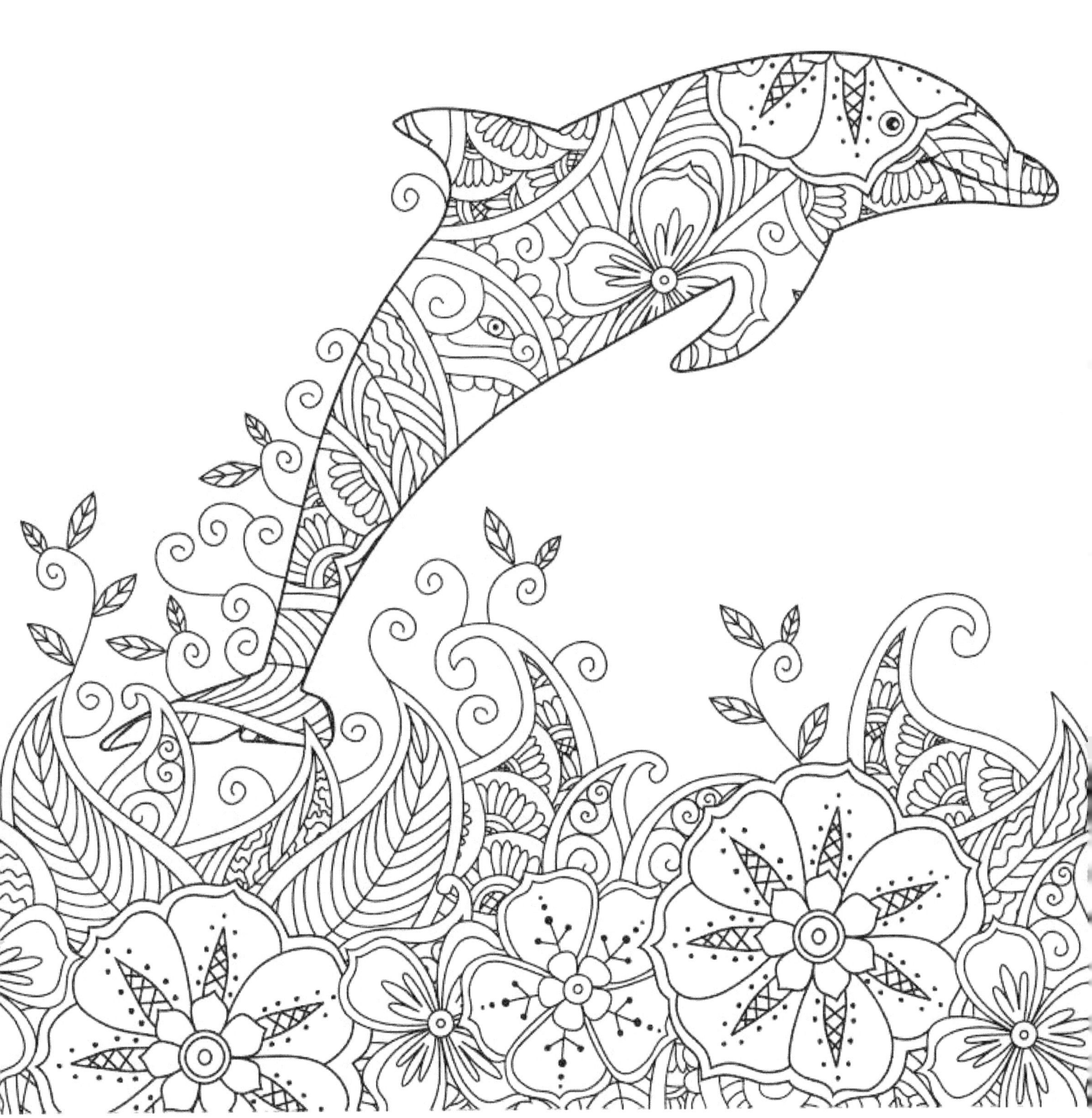

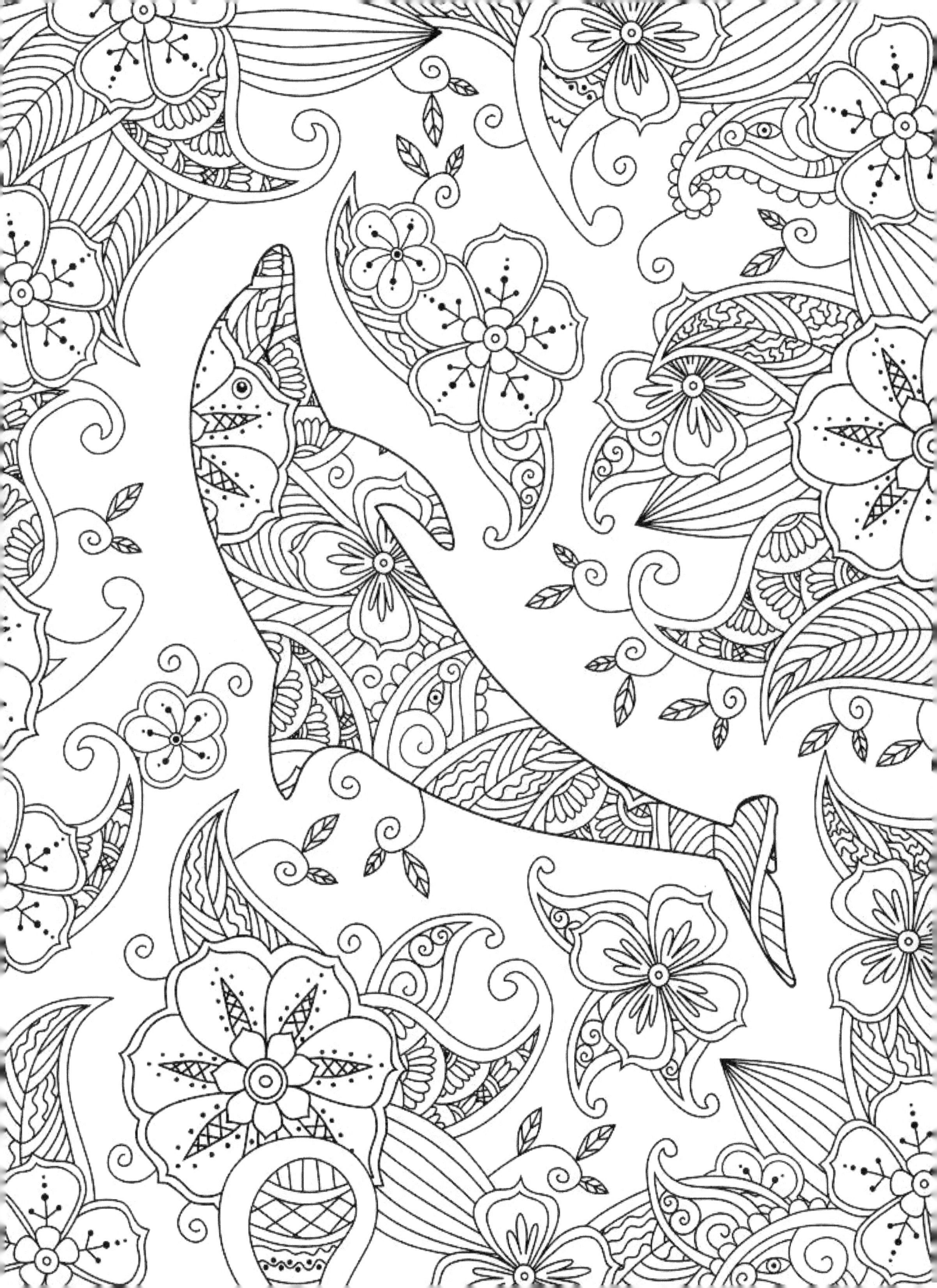

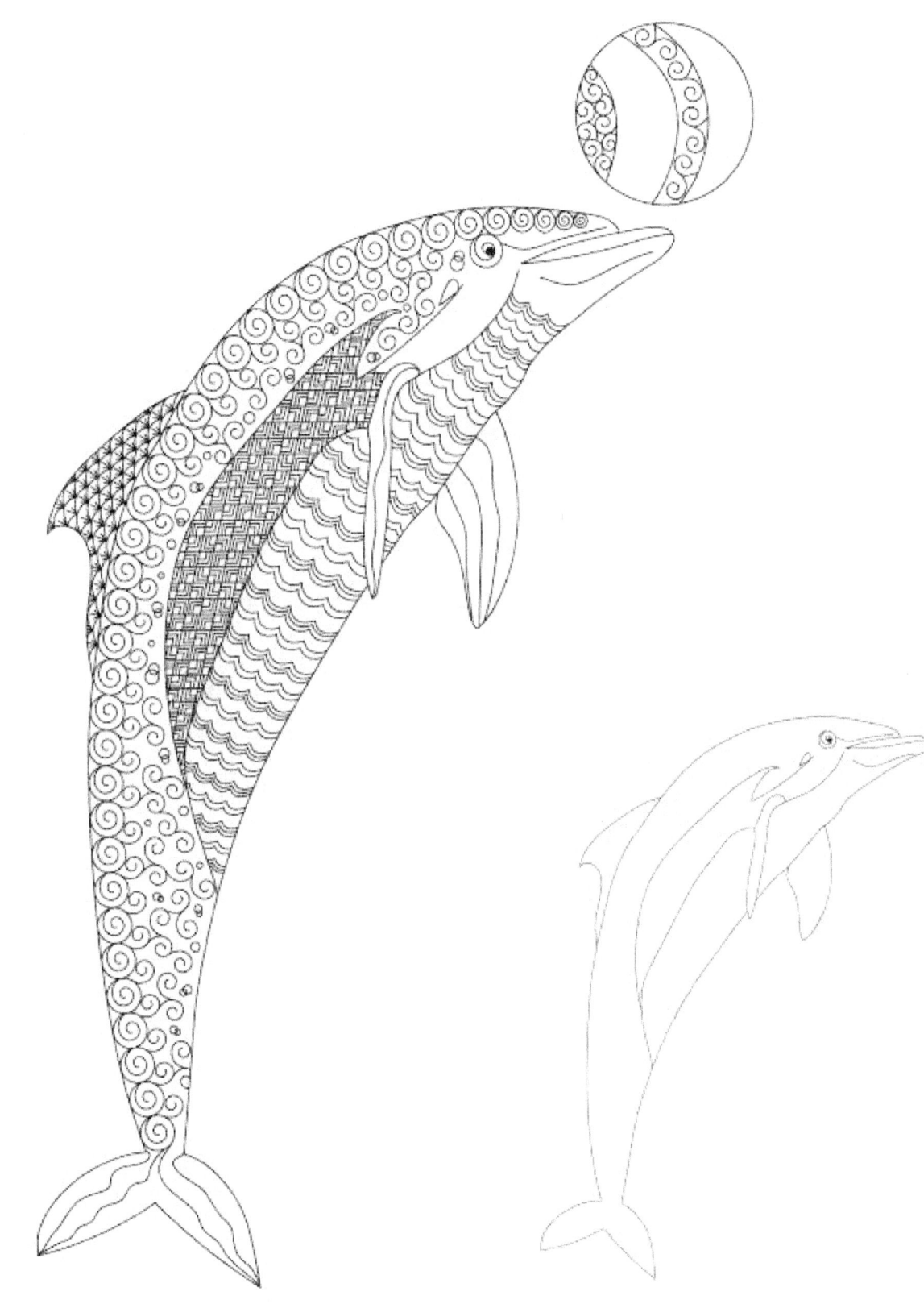

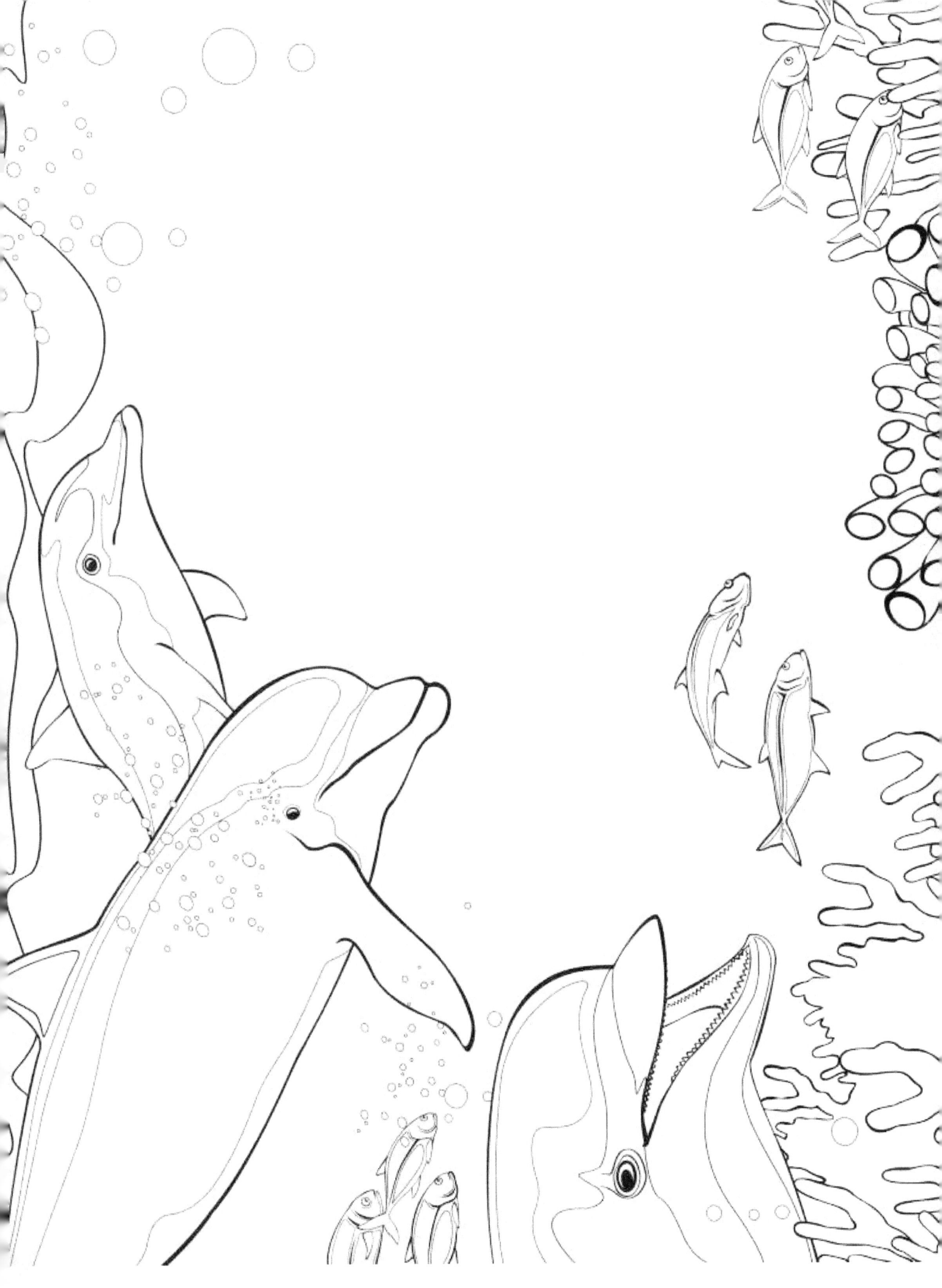

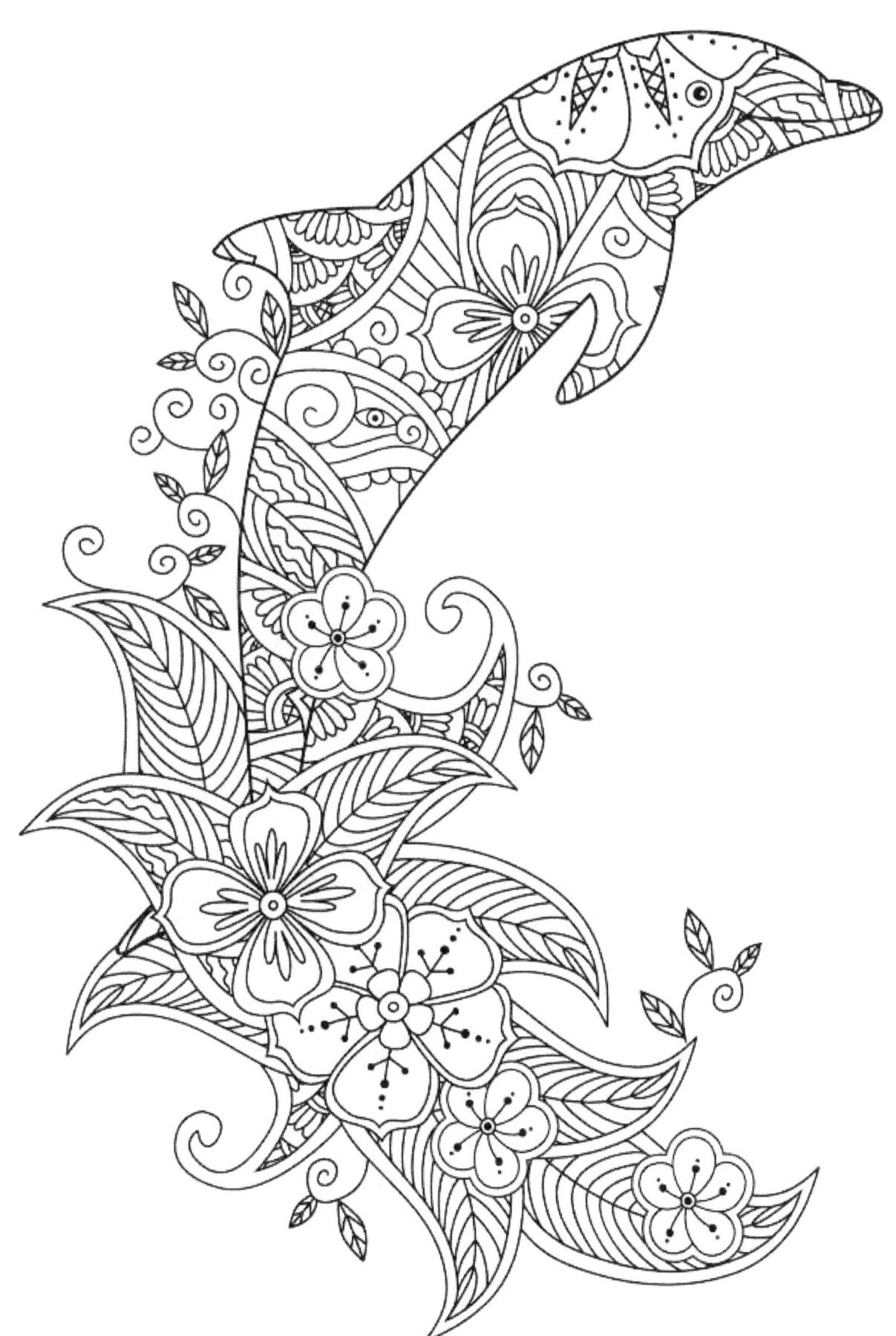

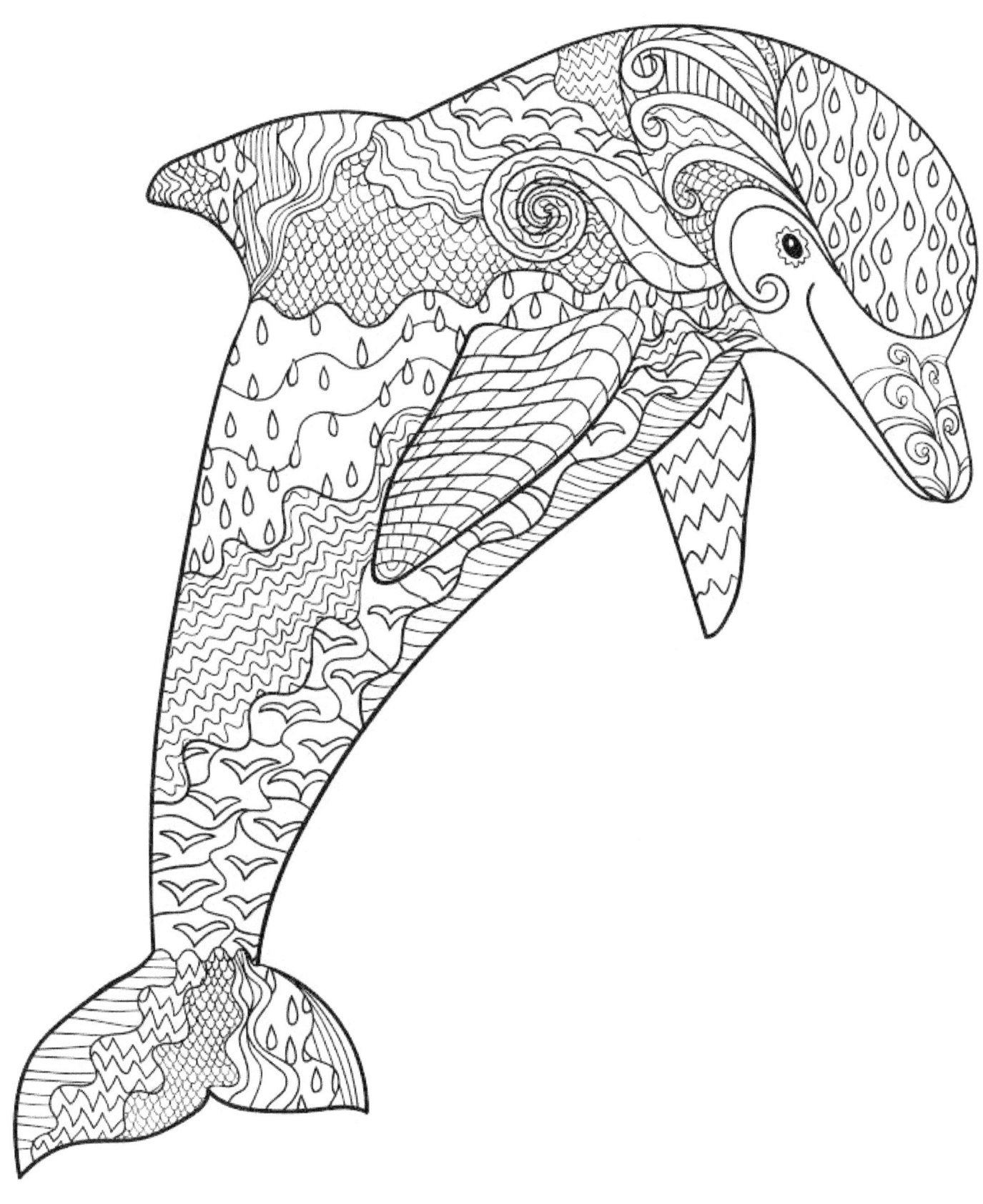

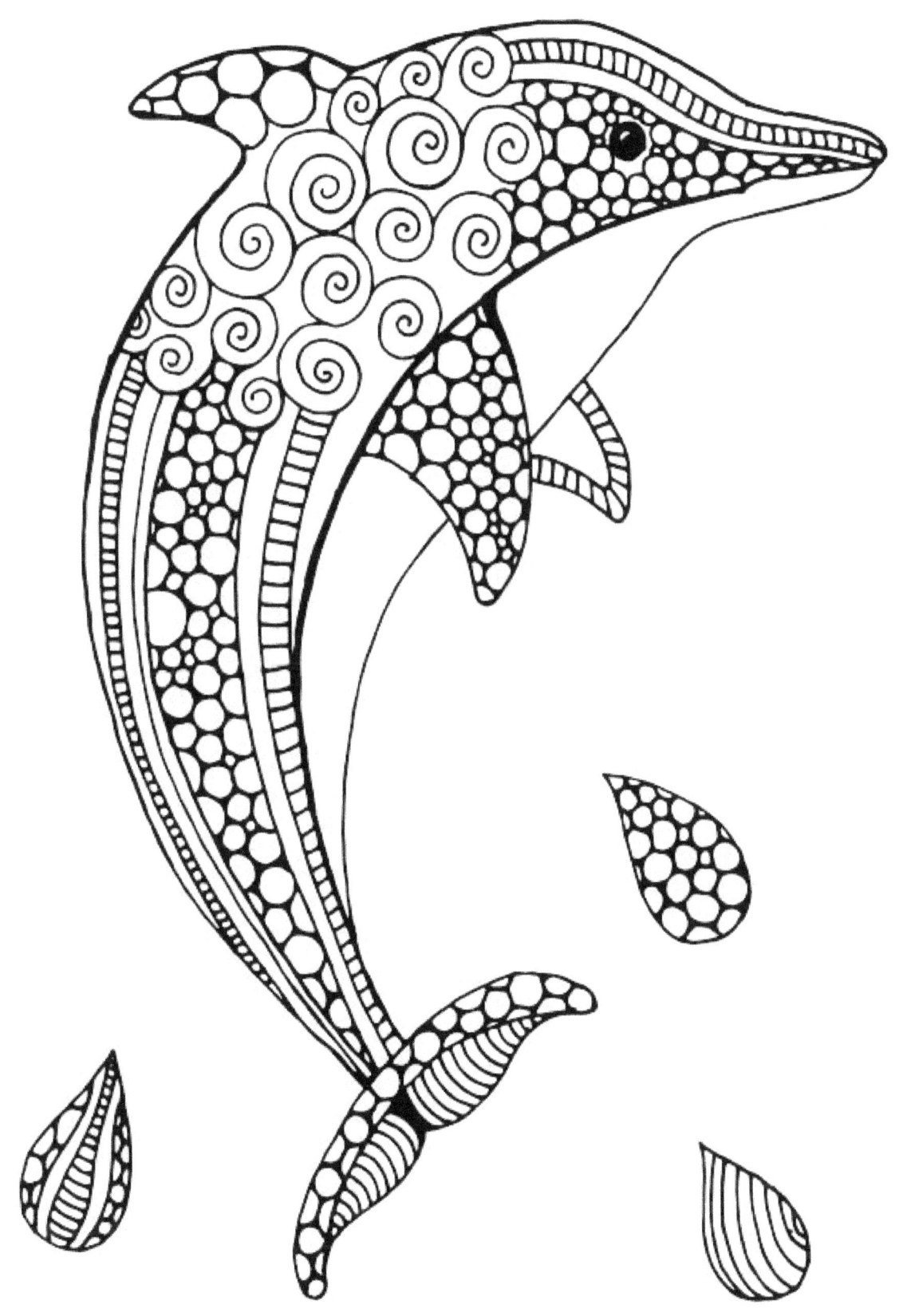

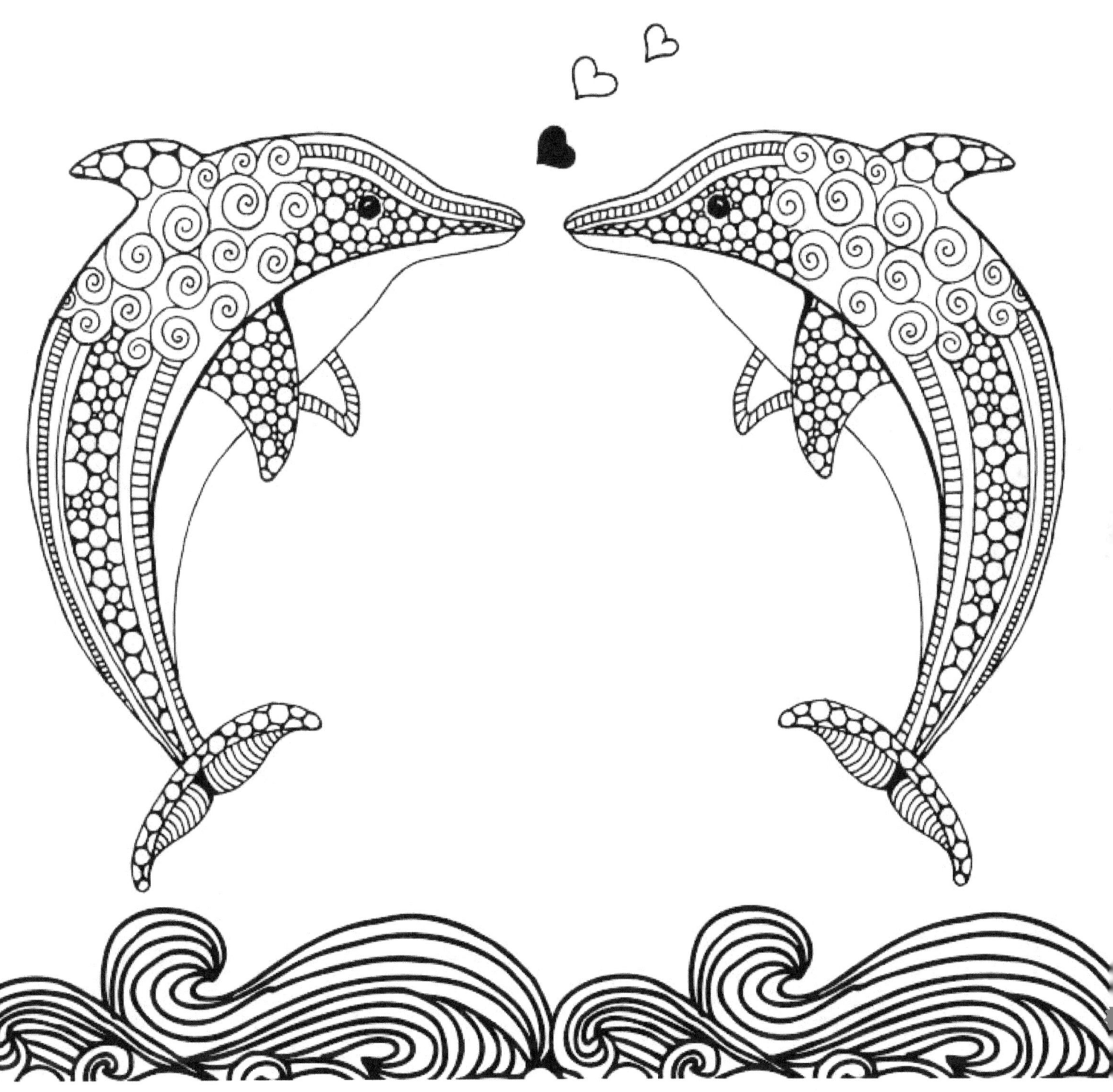

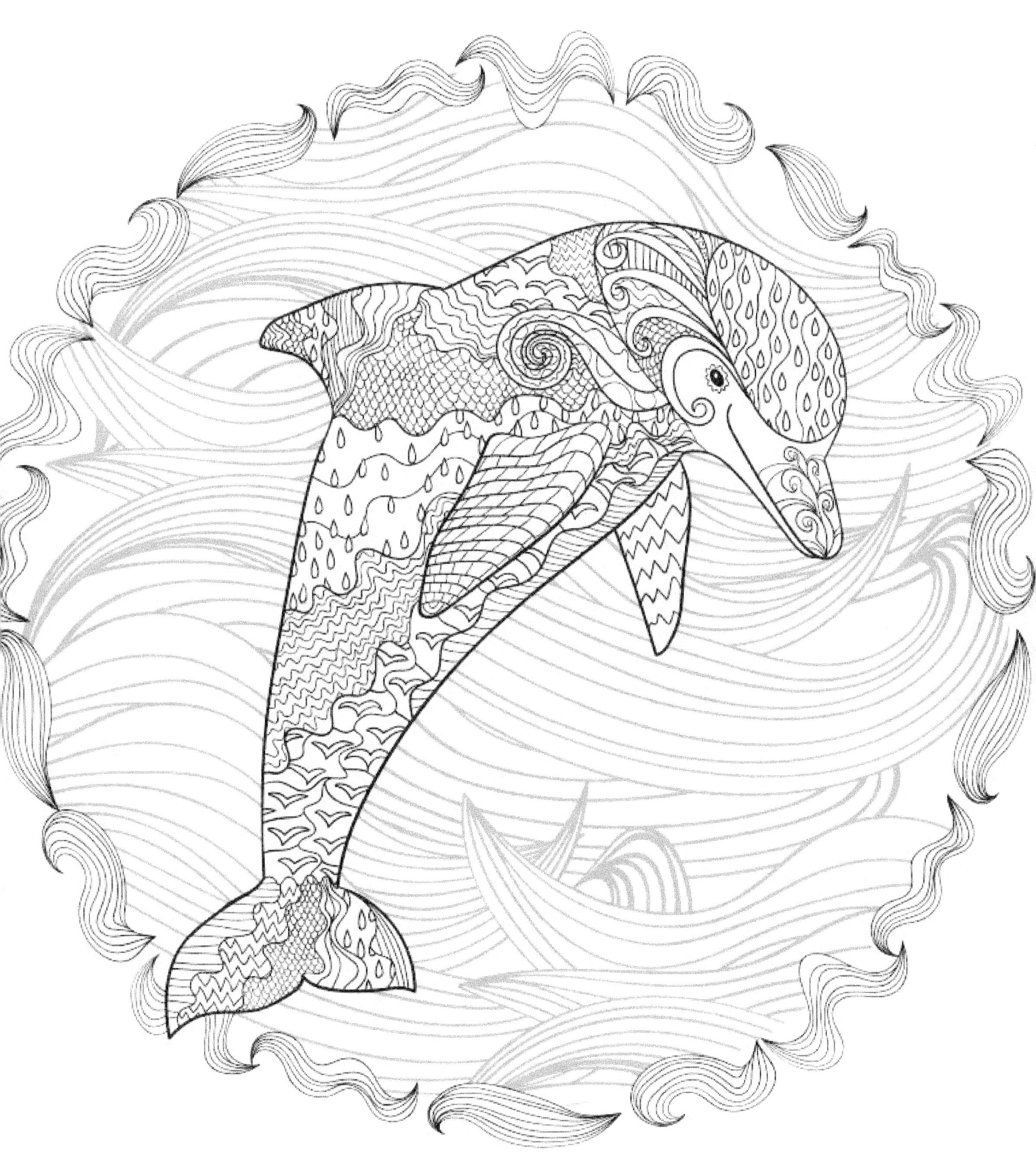

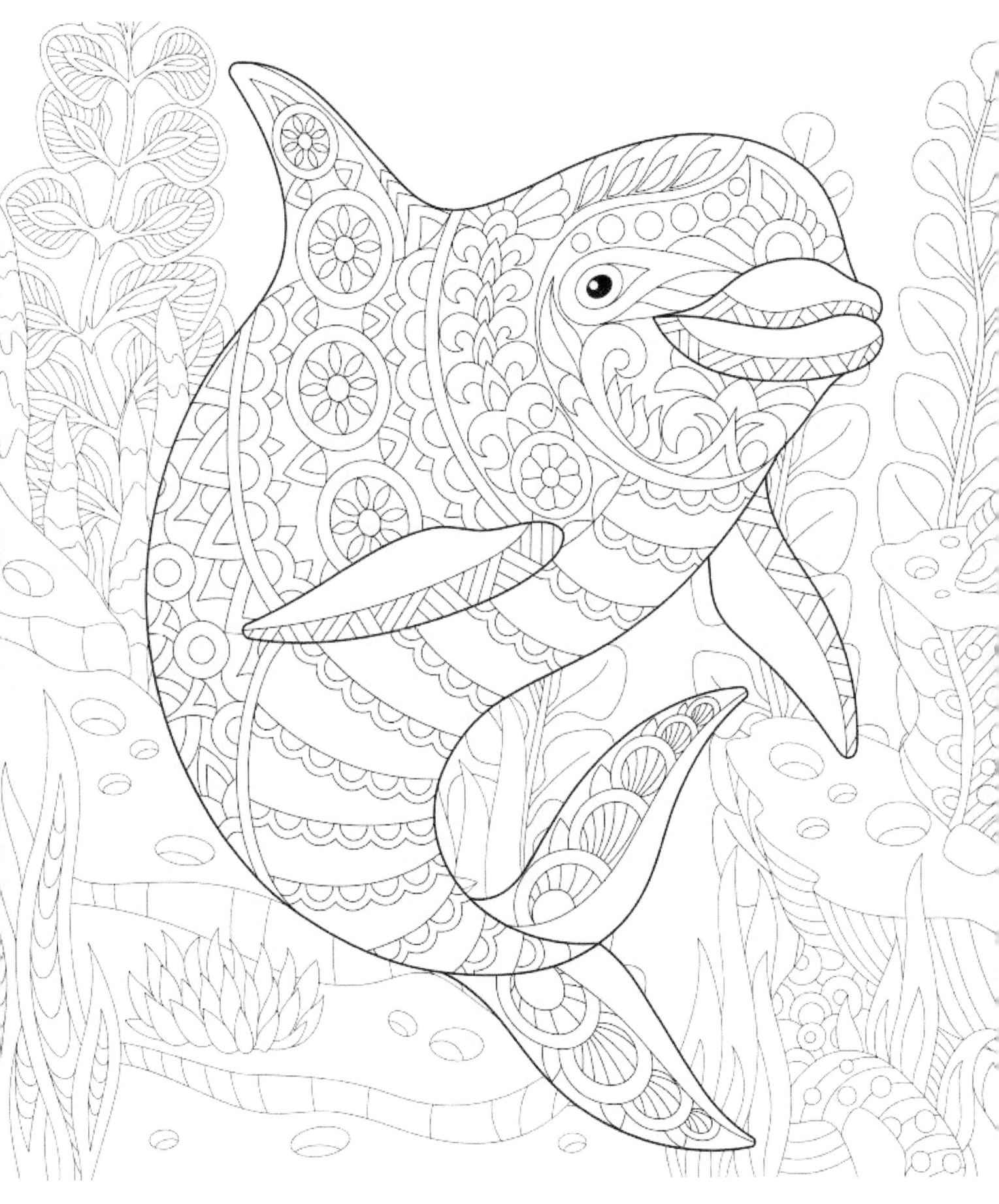

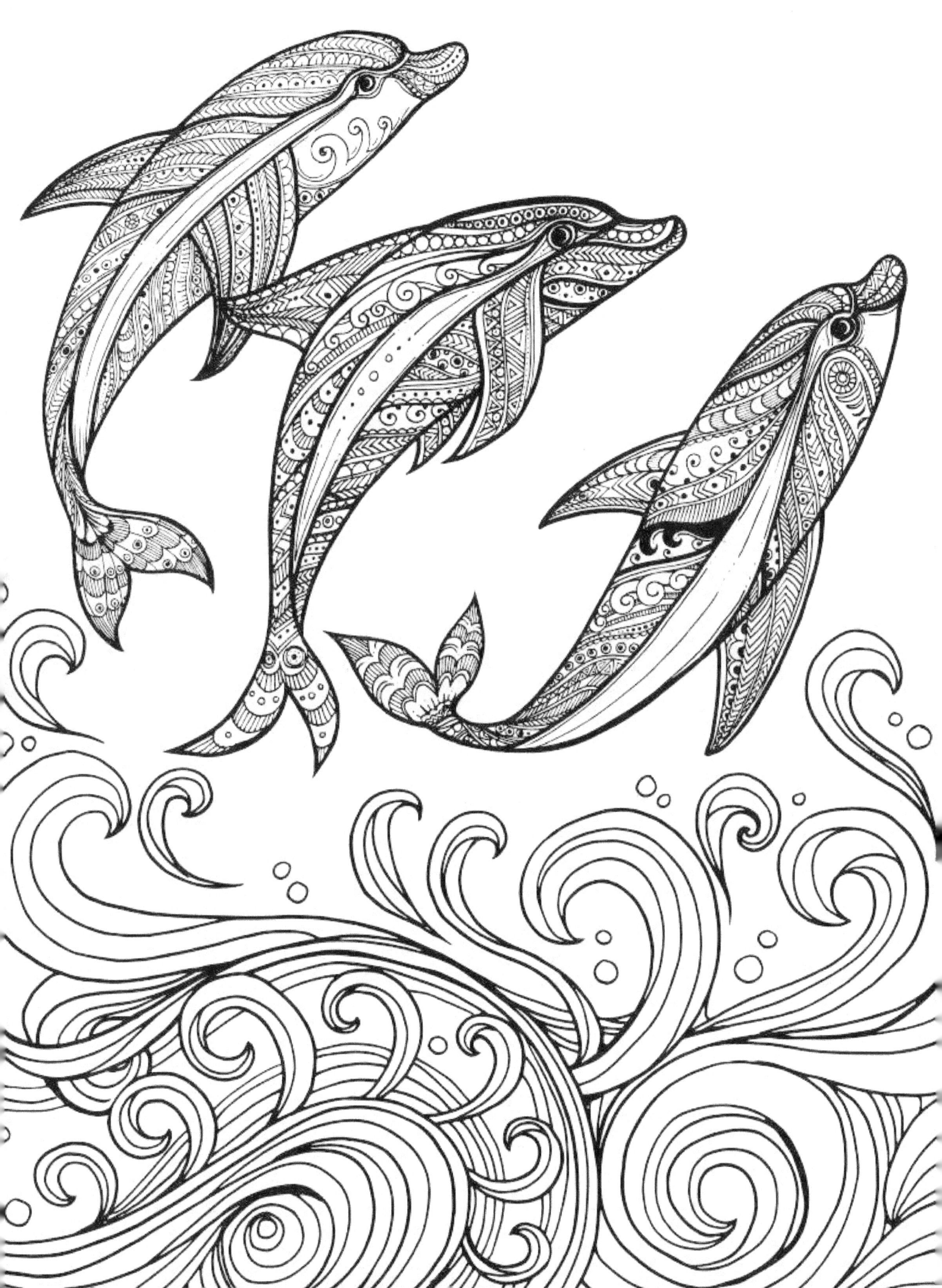

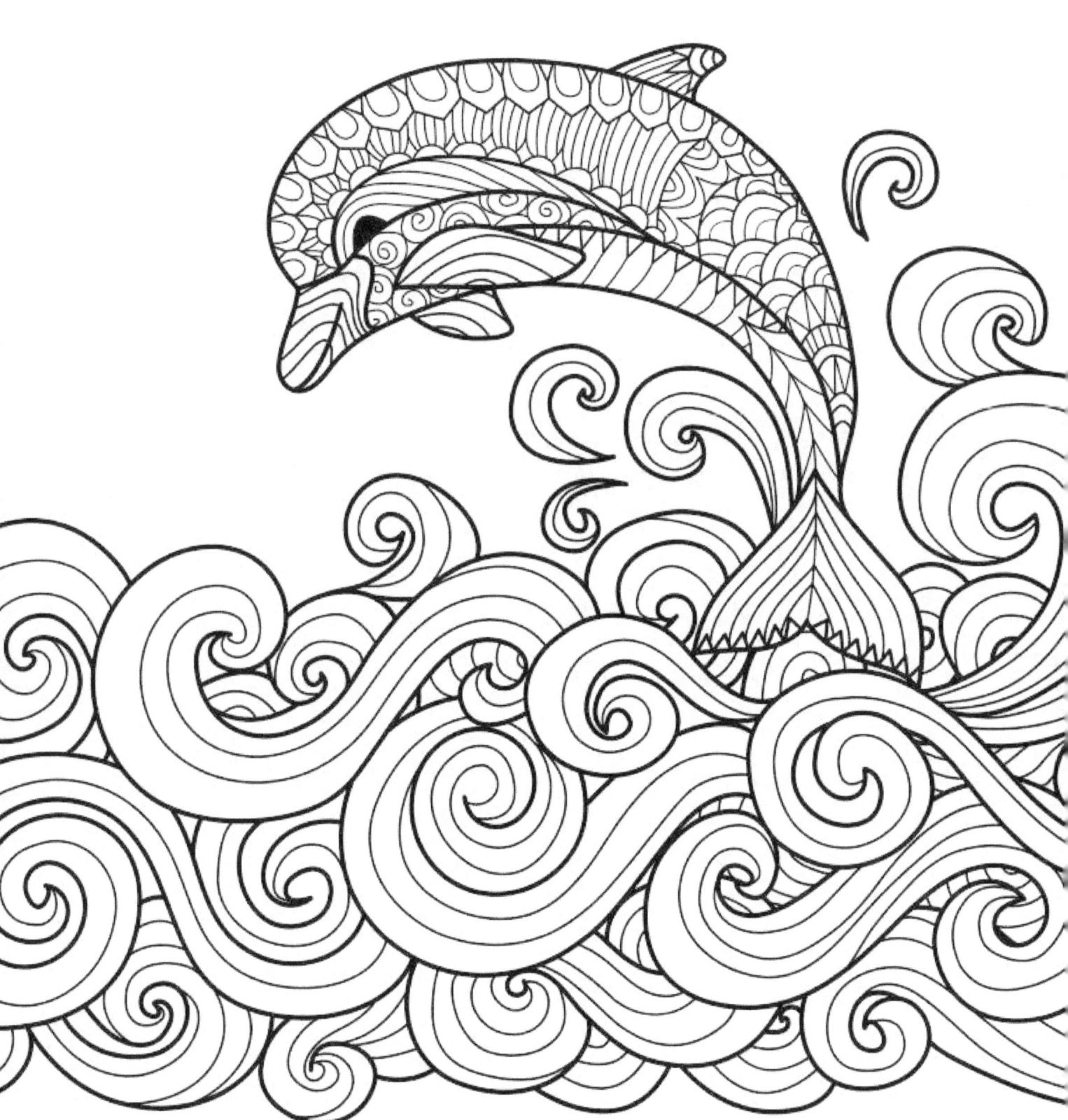

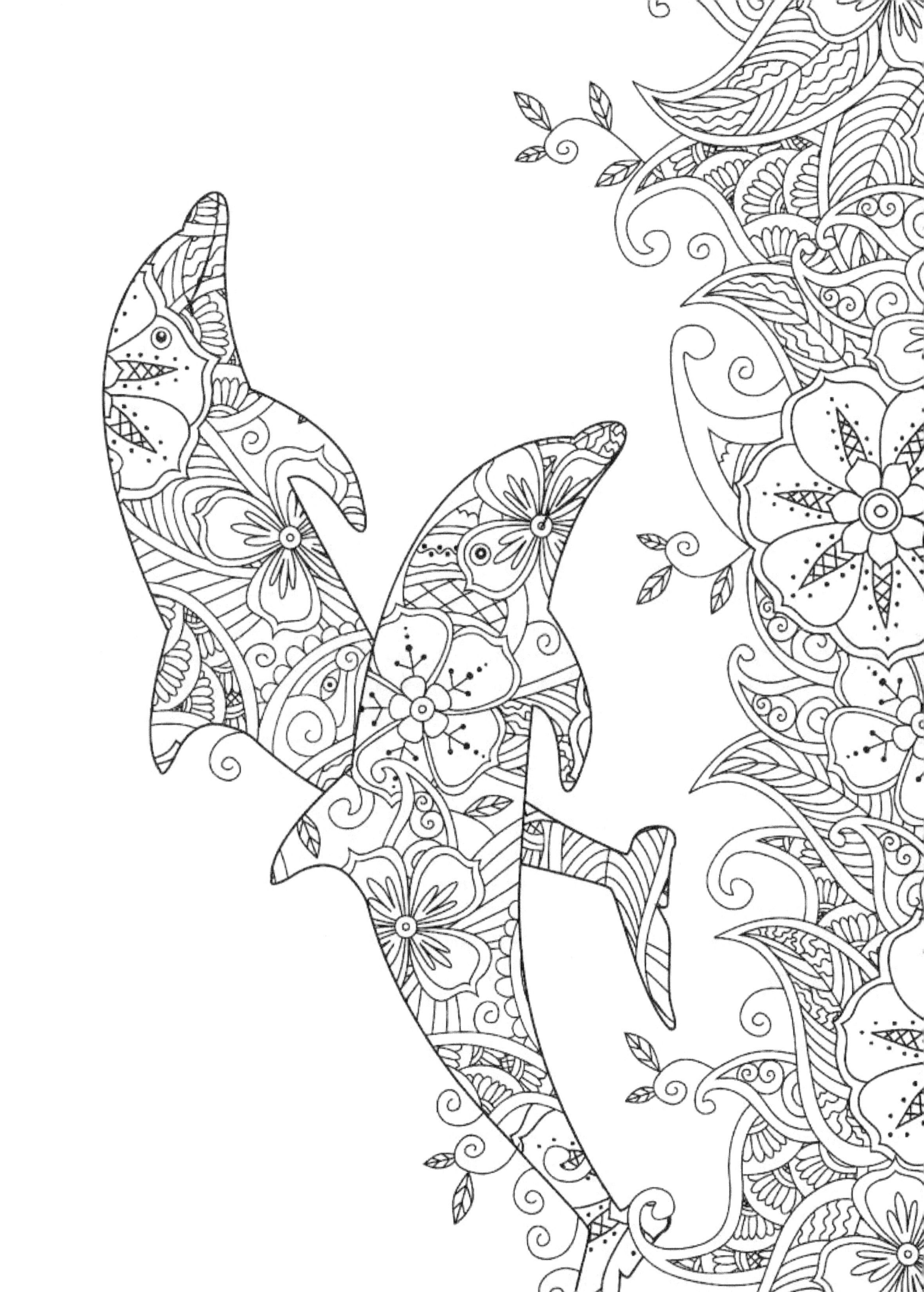

Free Surprise Bonus Whales Coloring Pages. Enjoy!

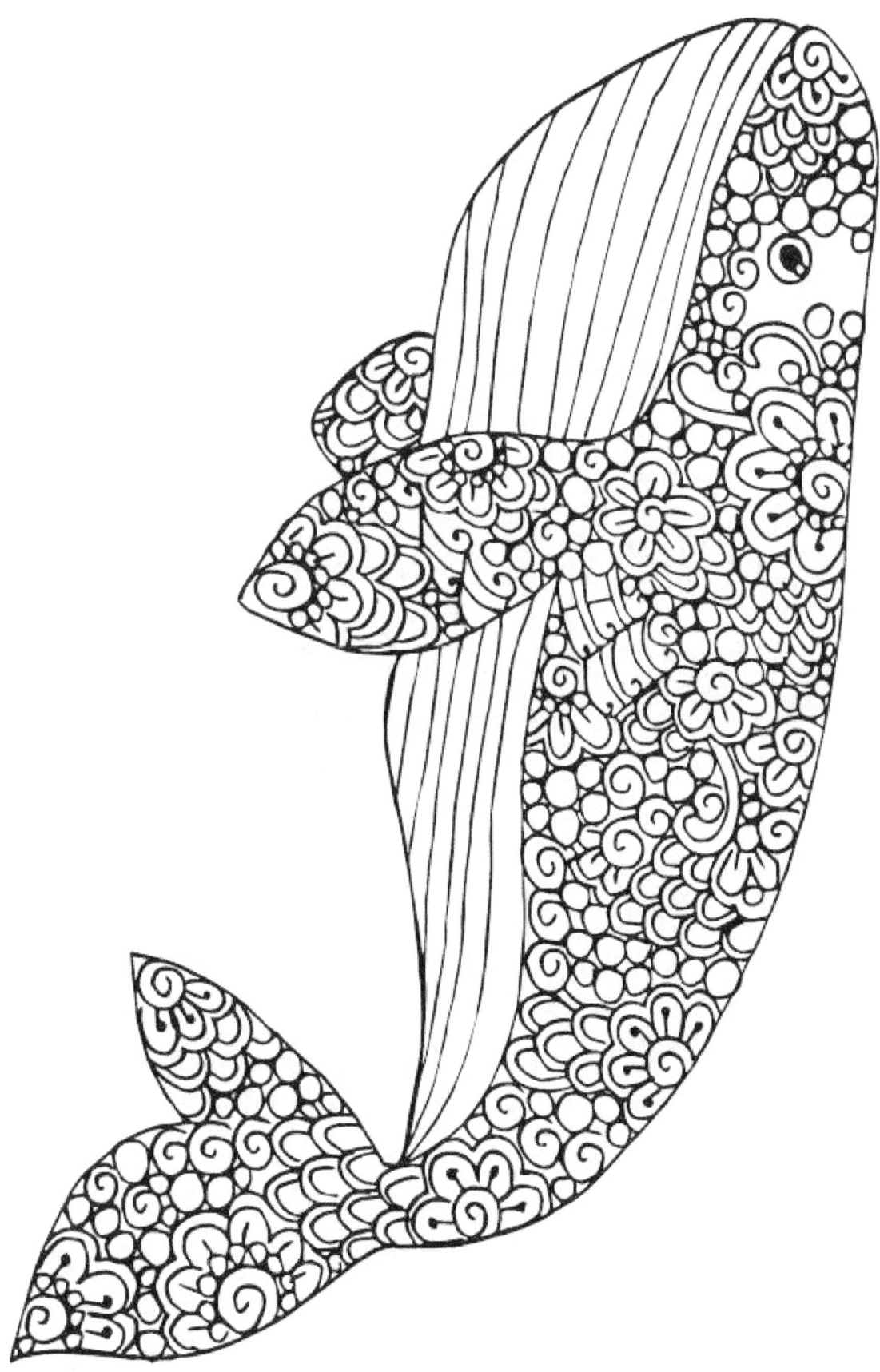

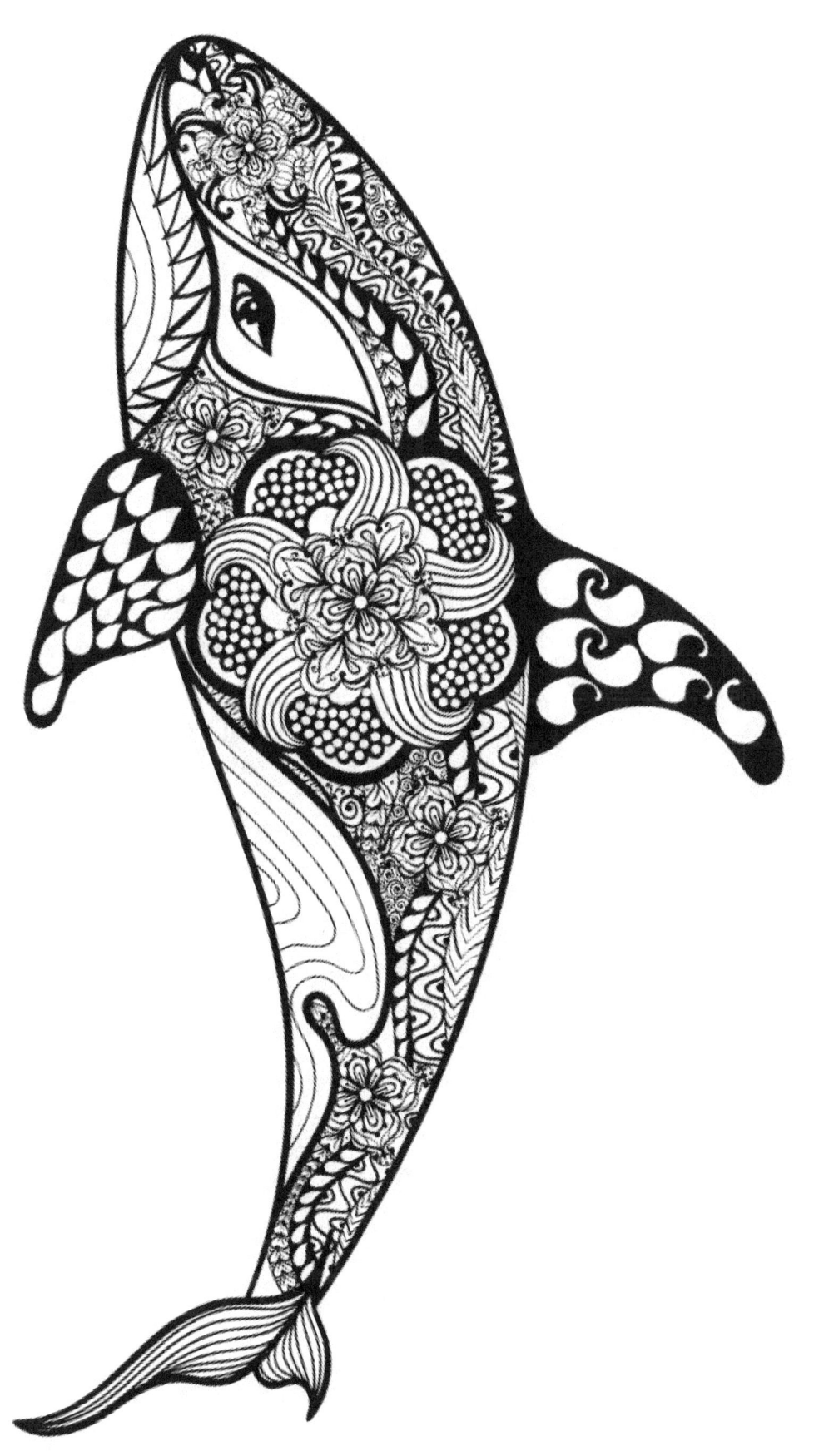

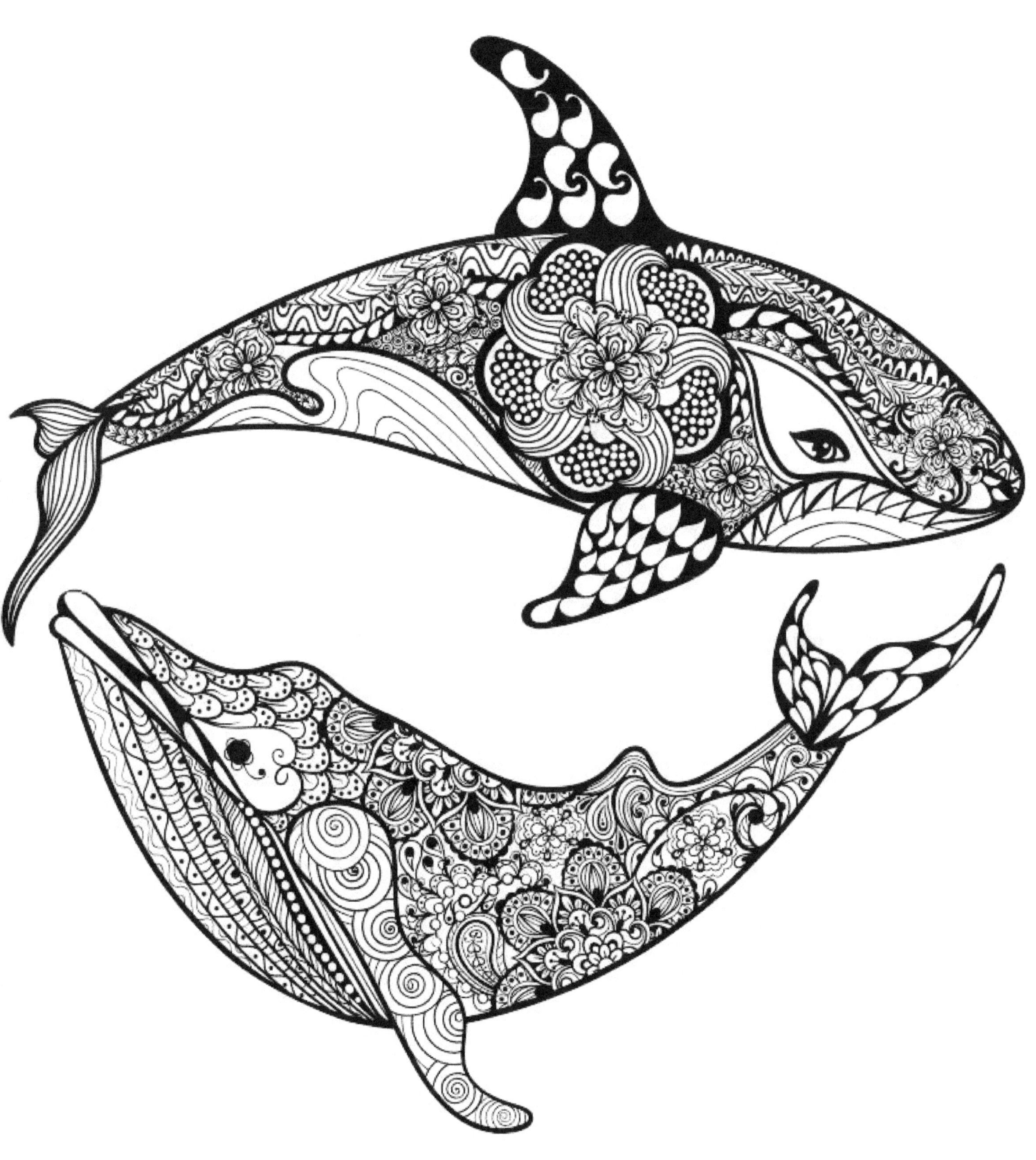

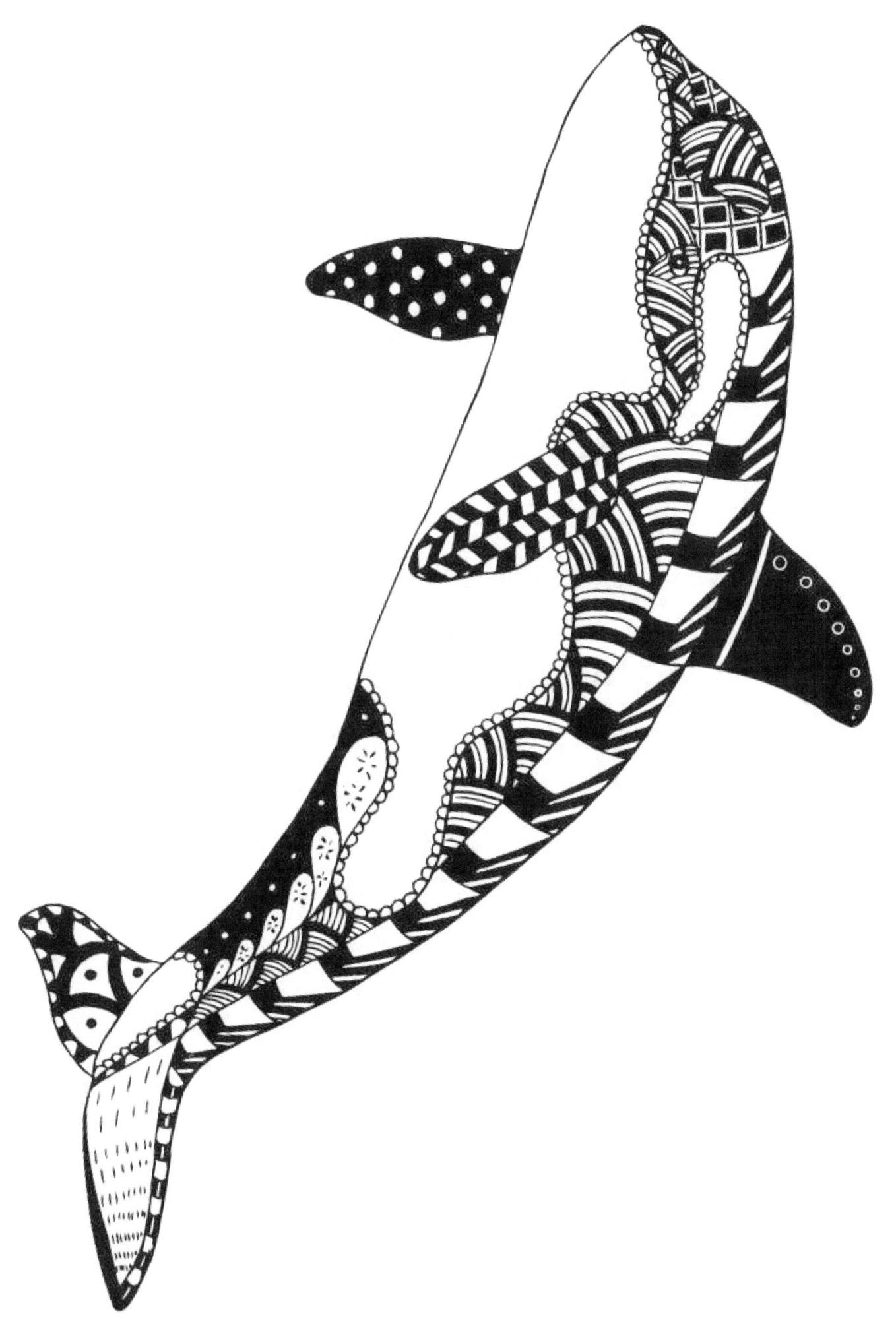

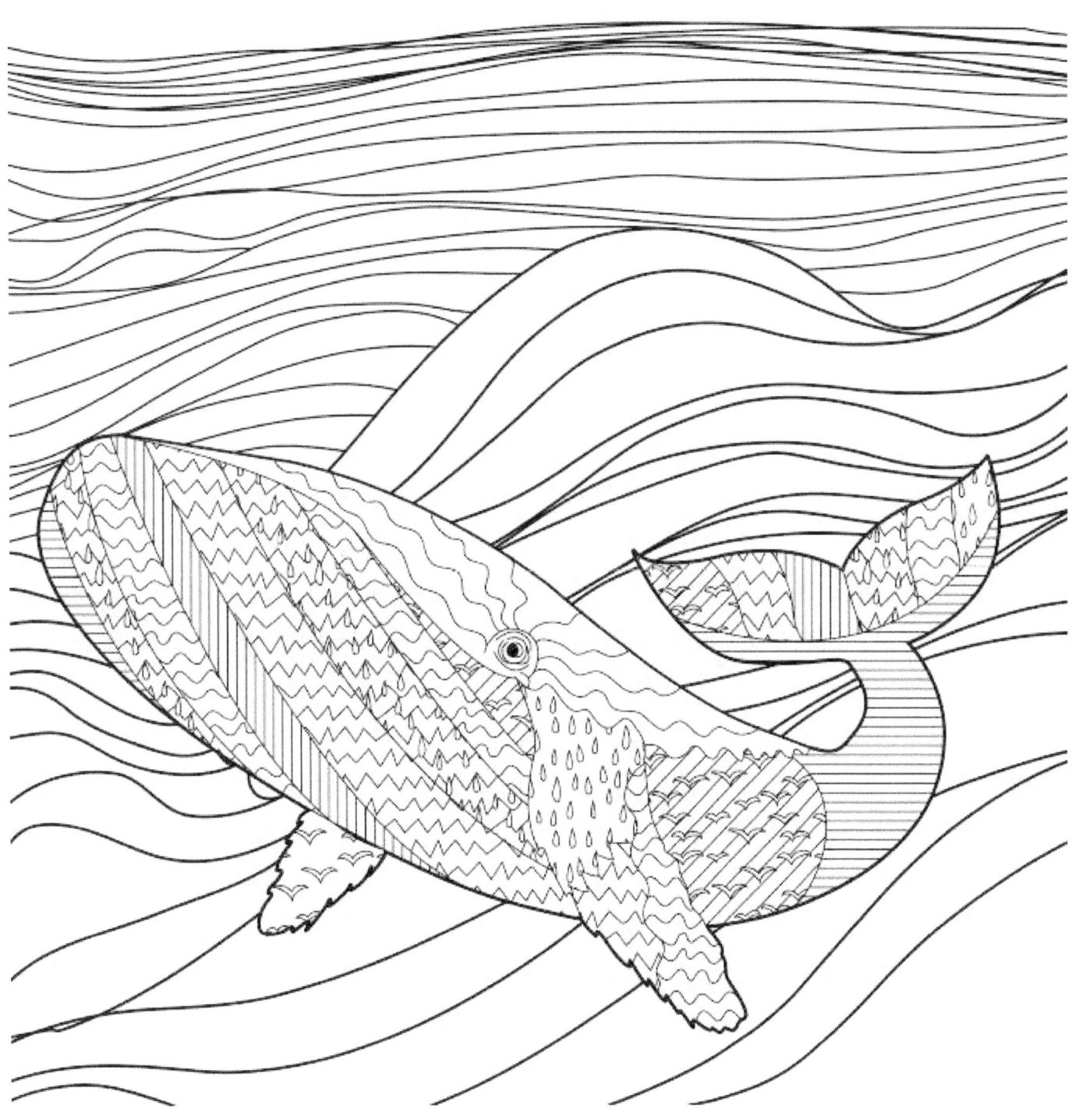

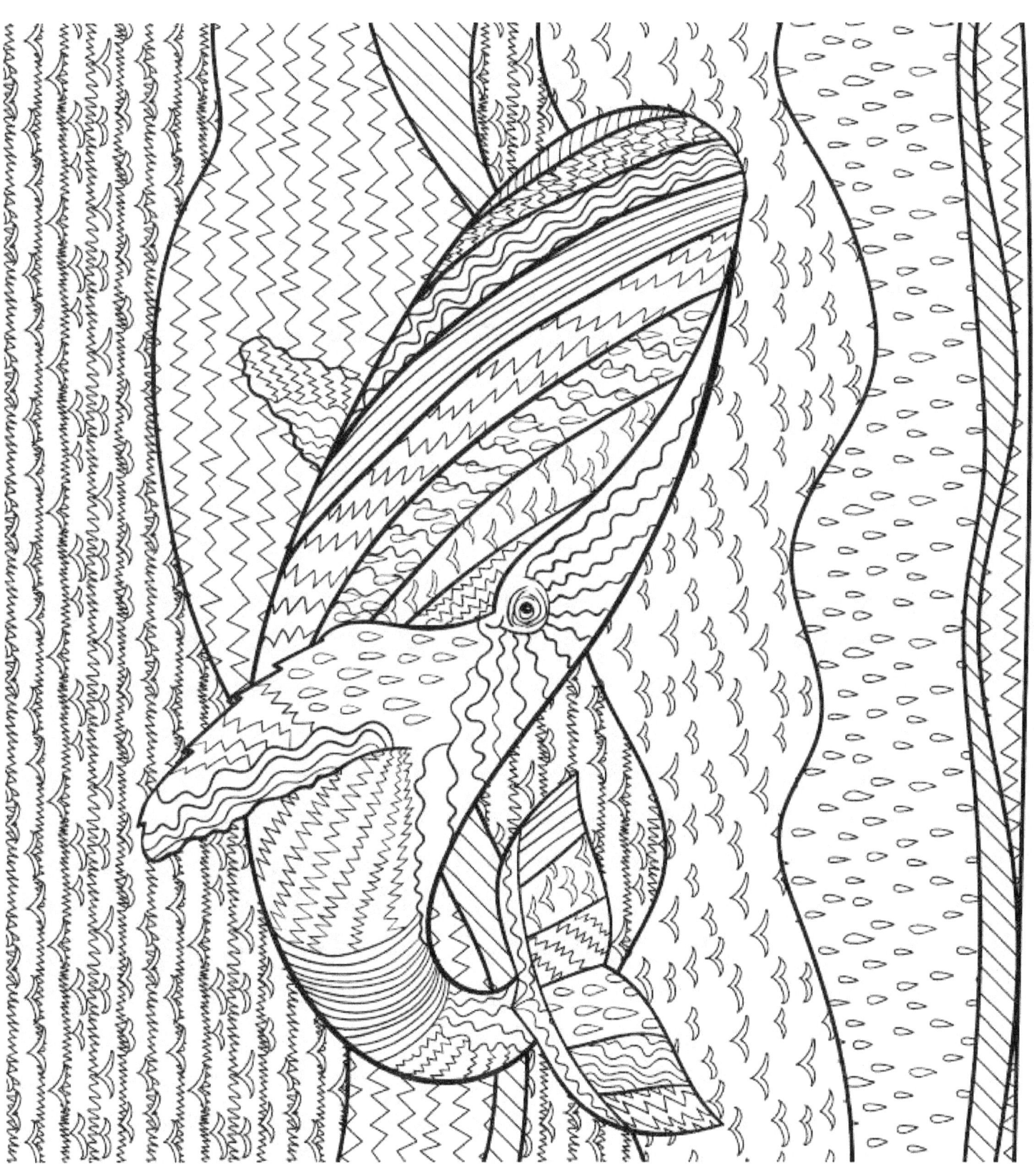

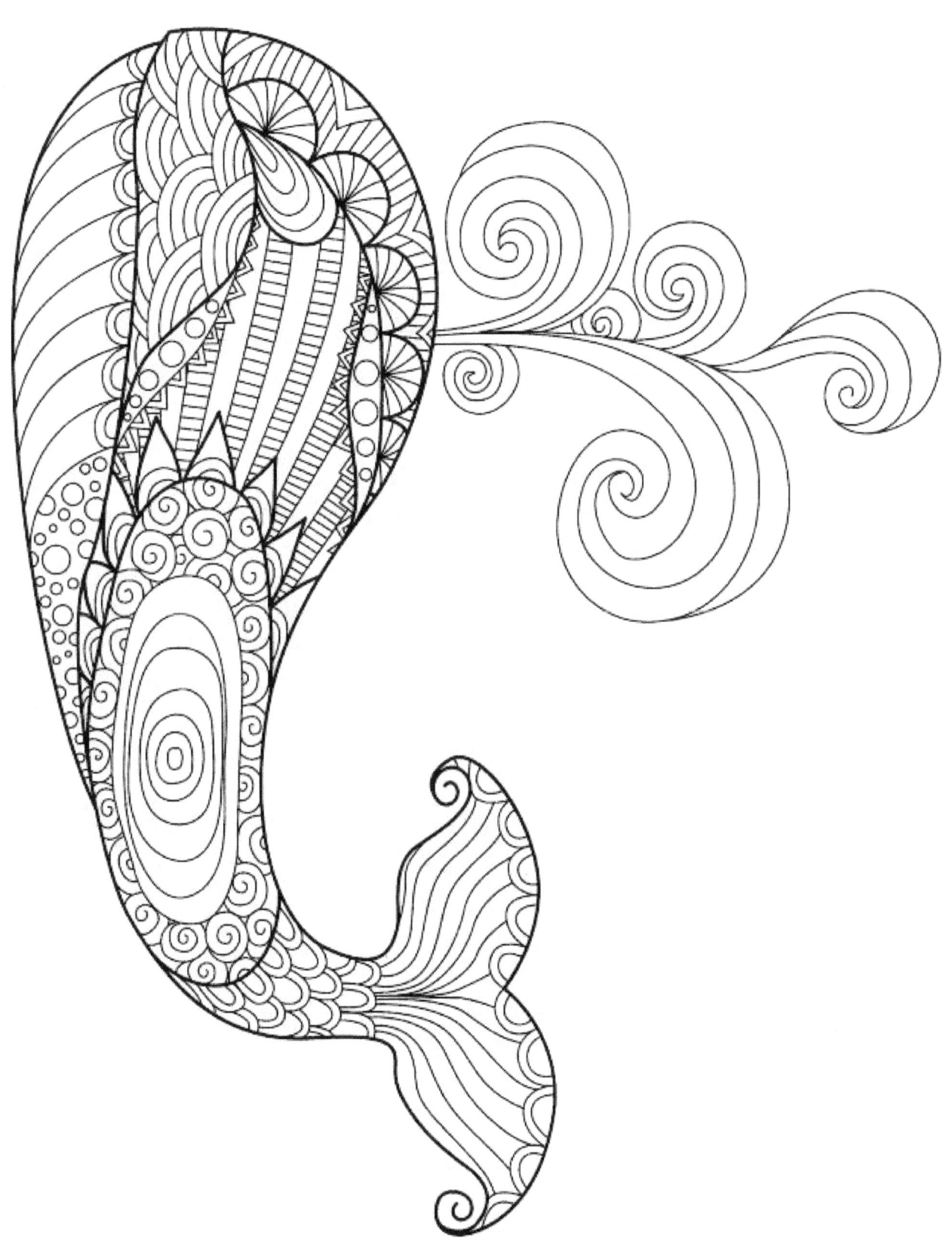

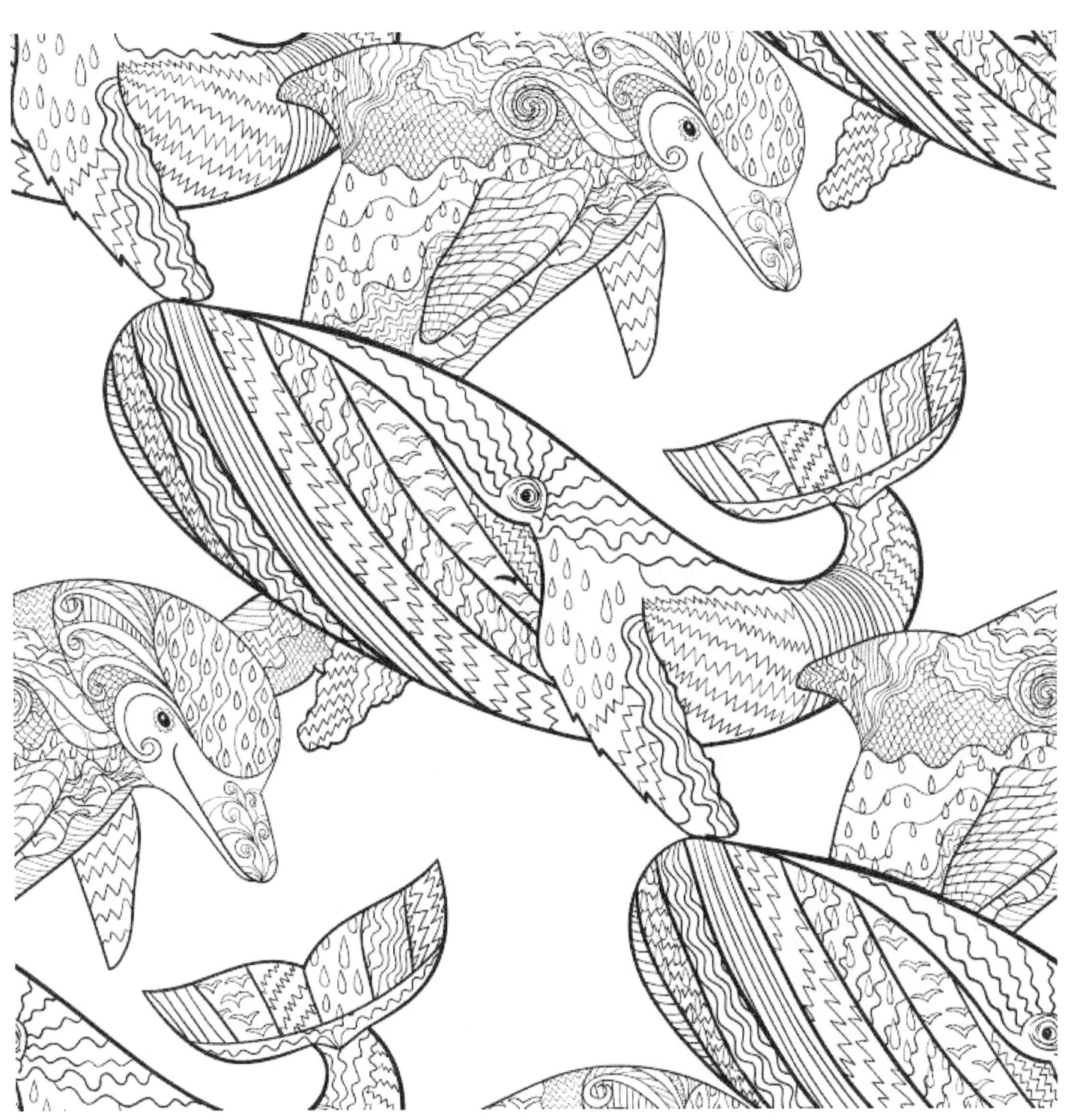

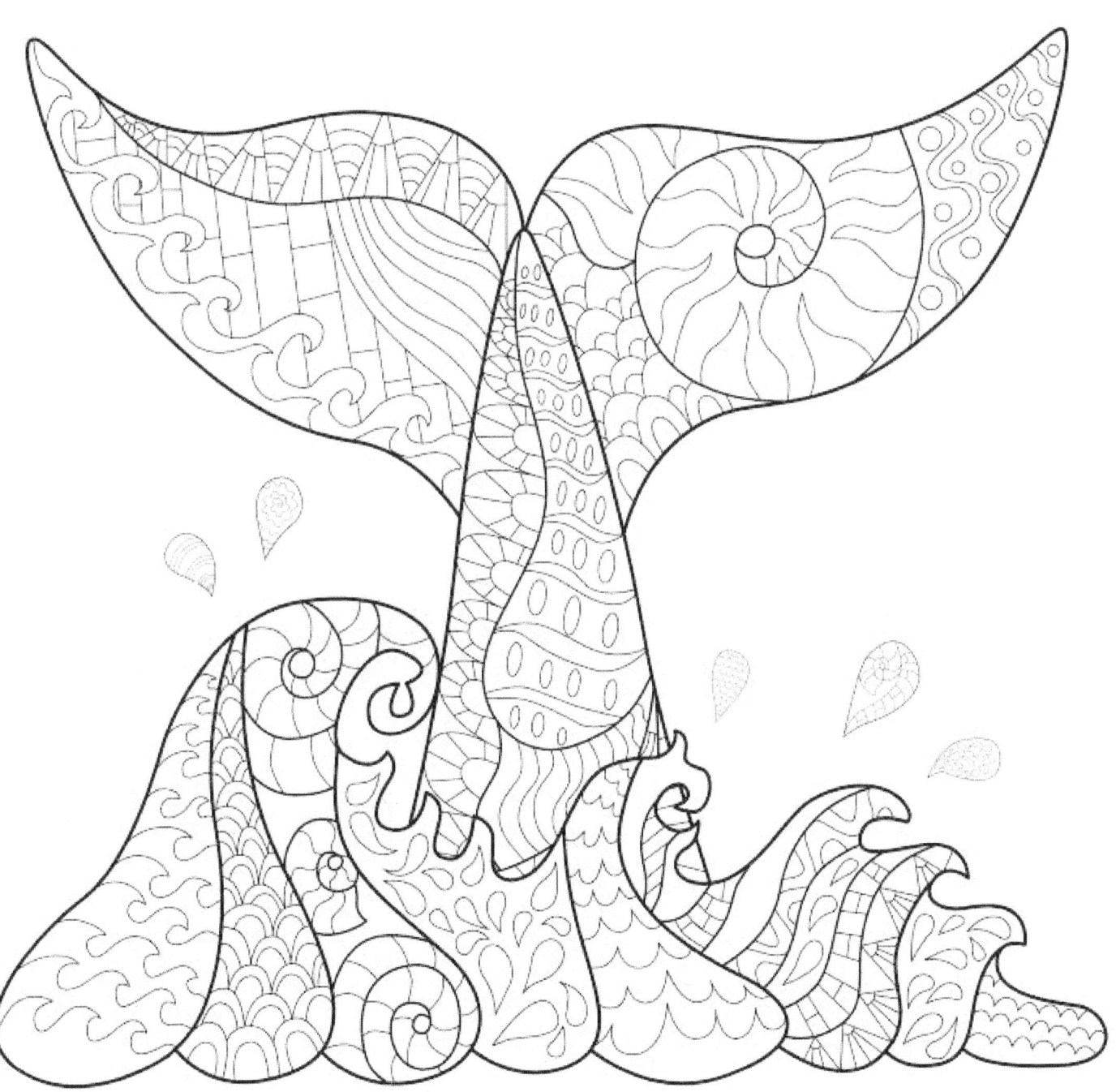

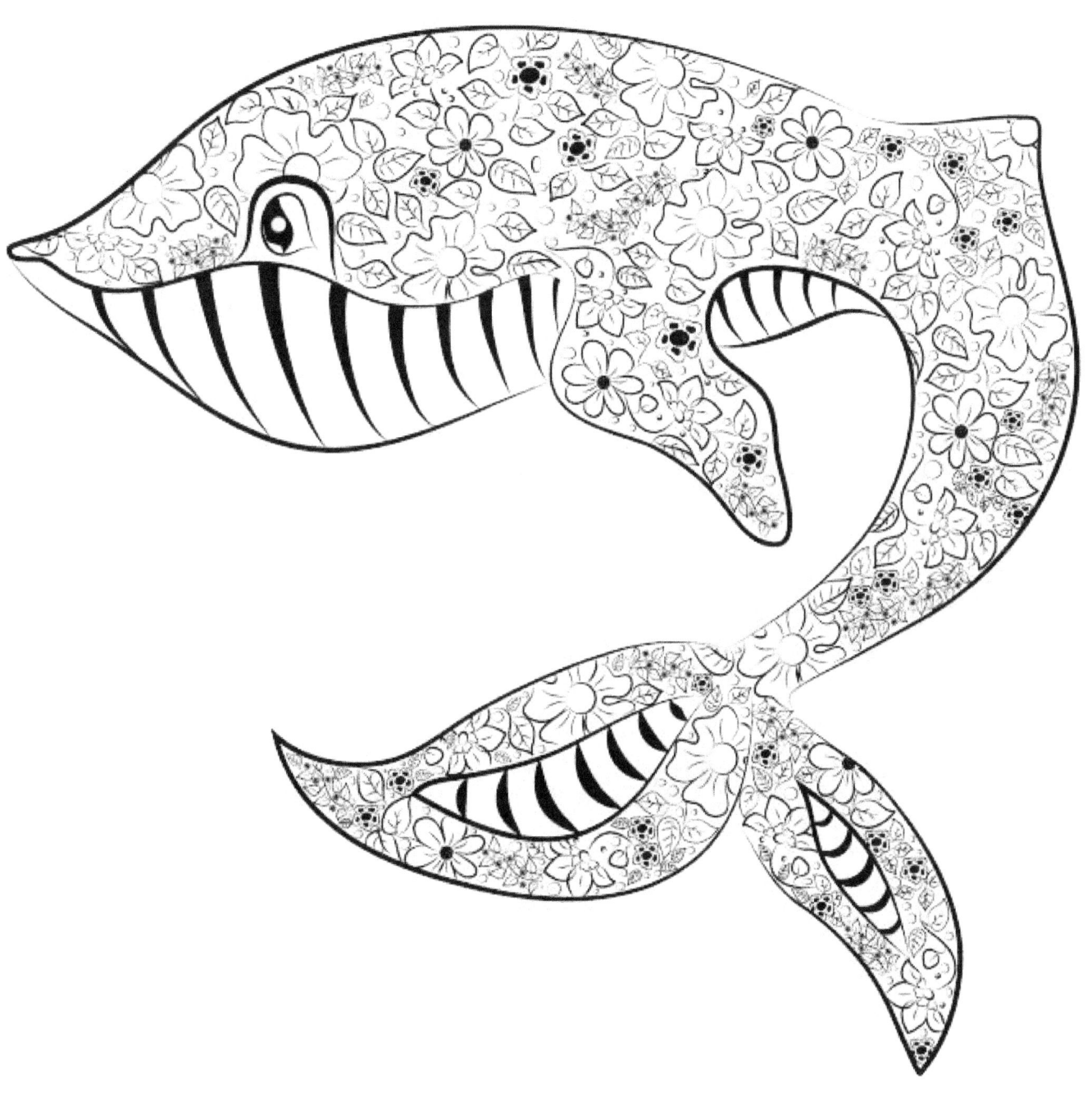

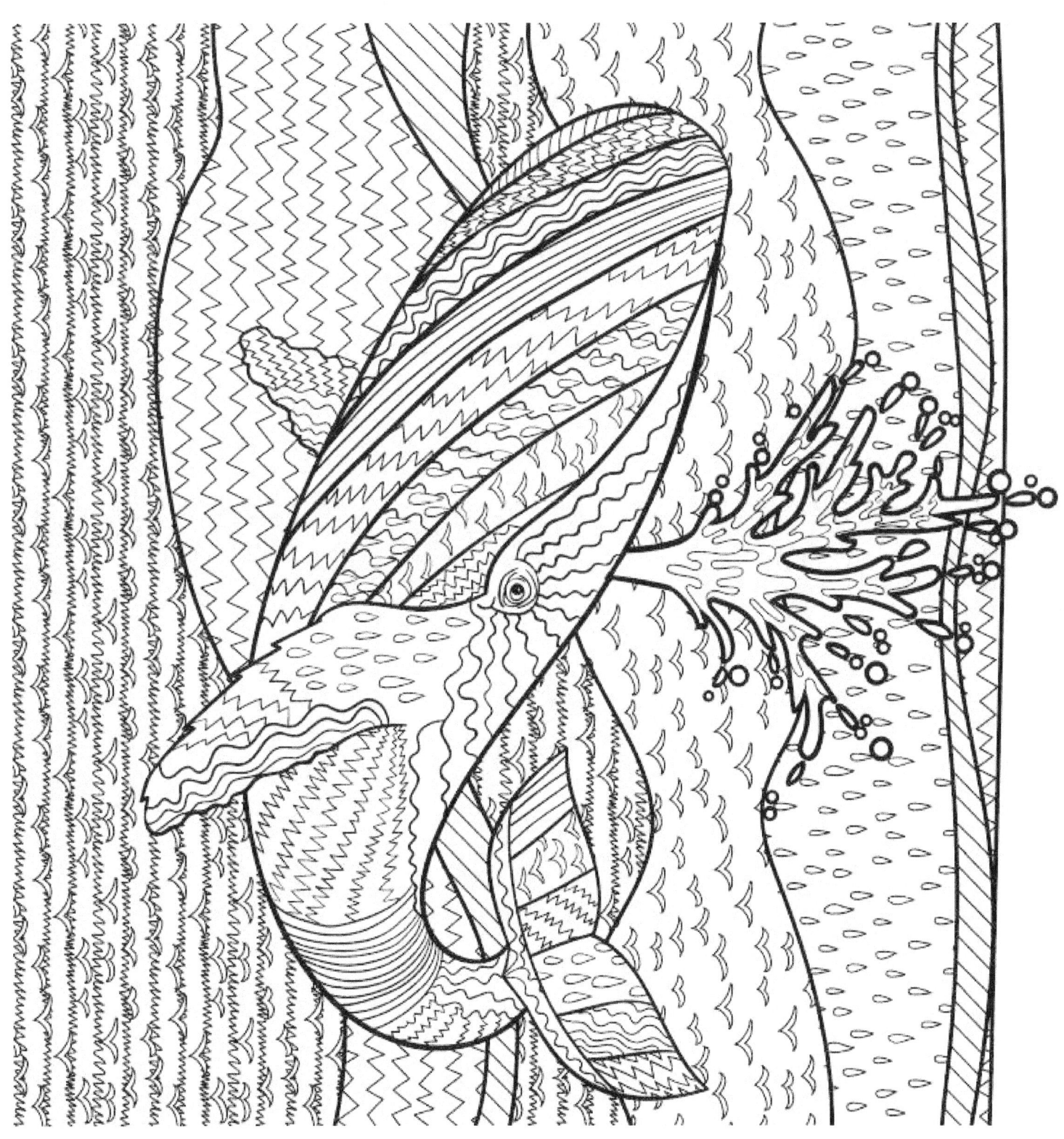

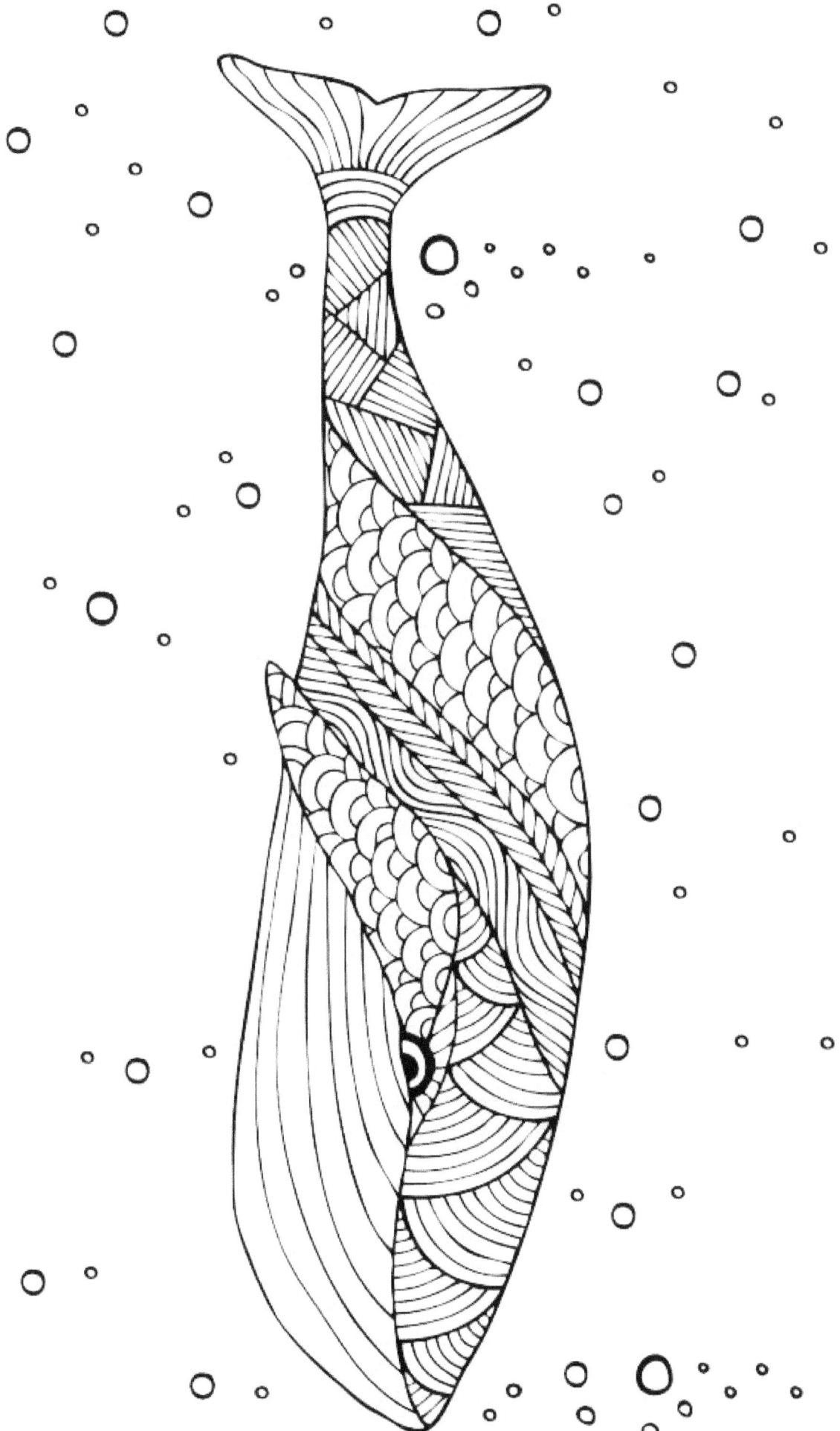

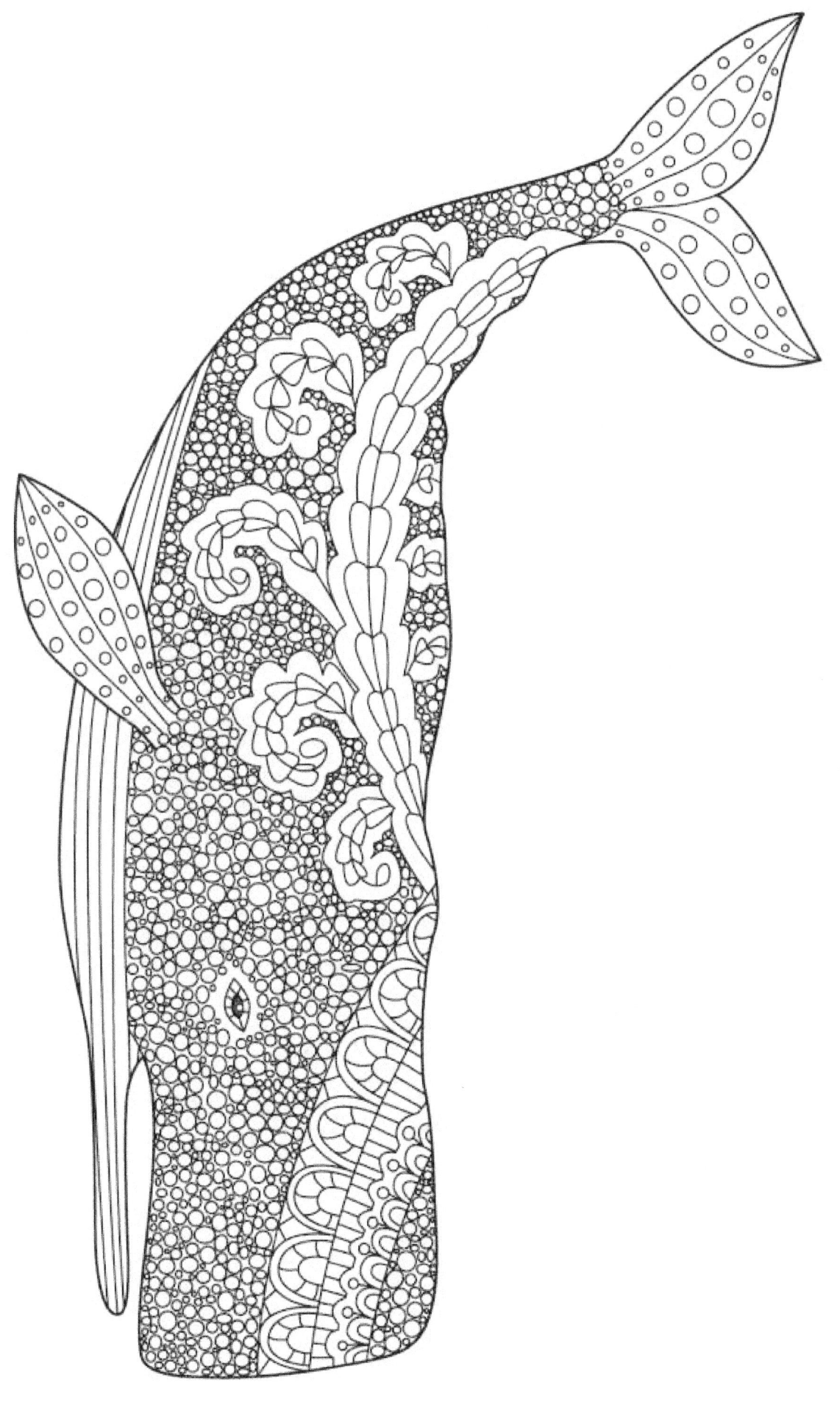

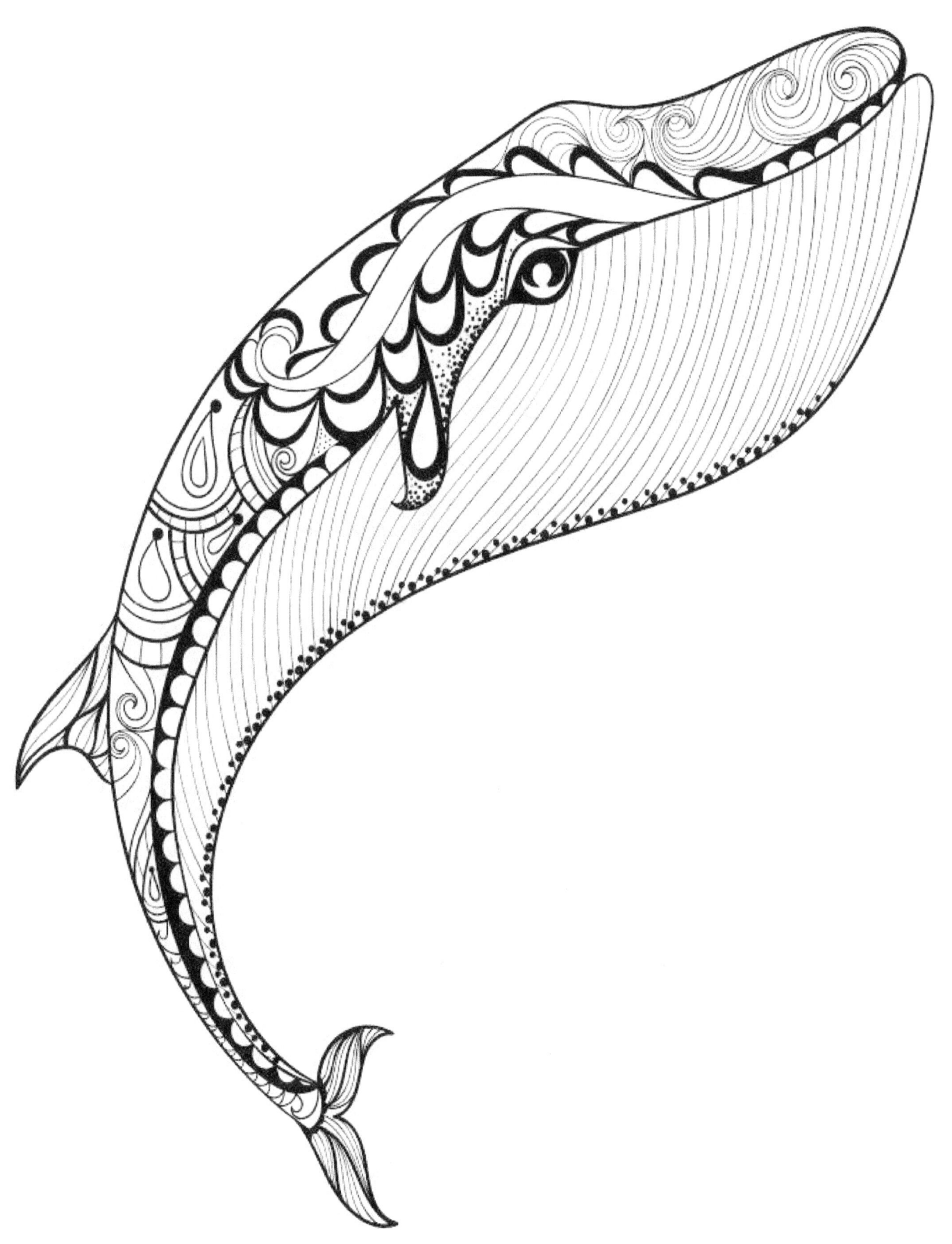

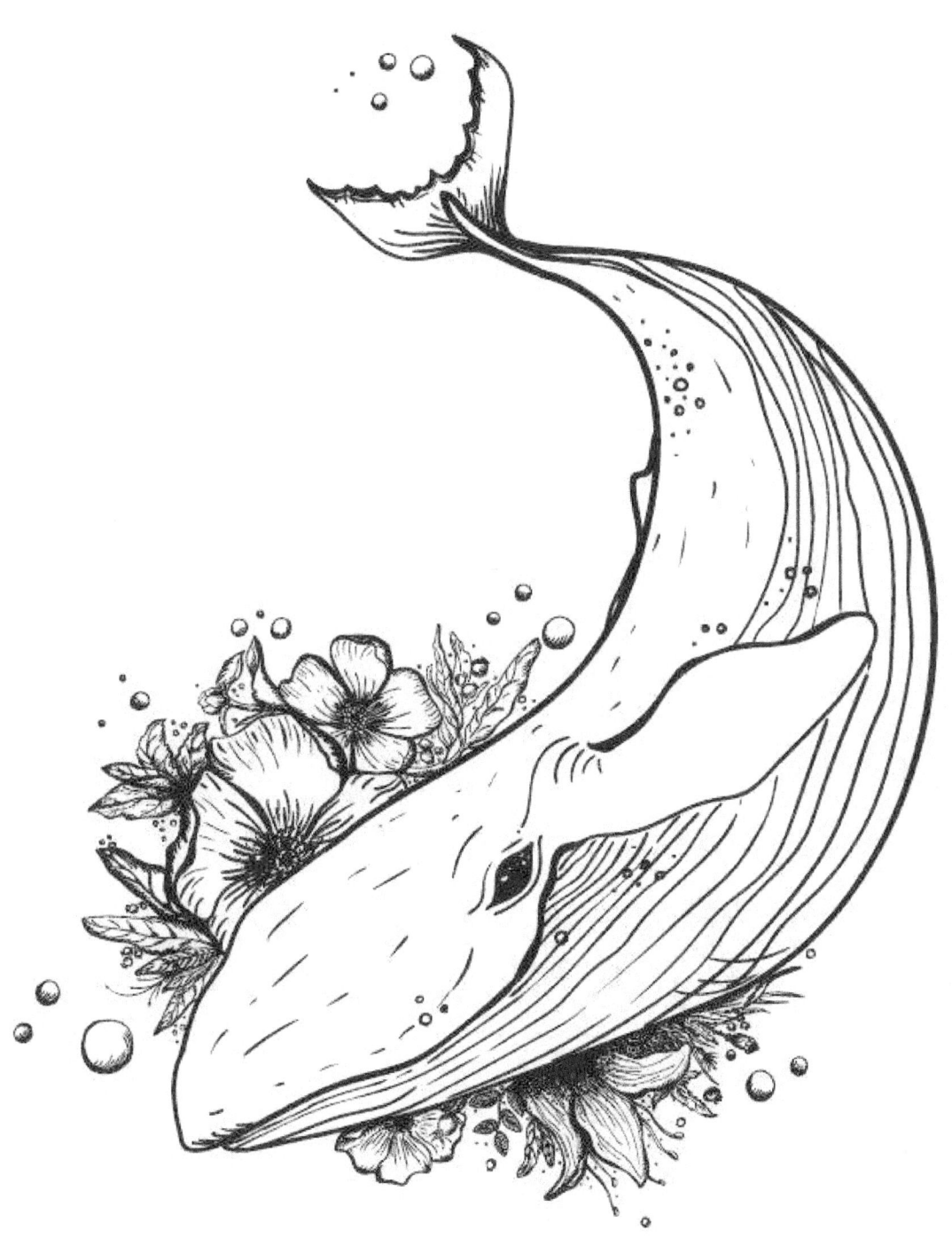

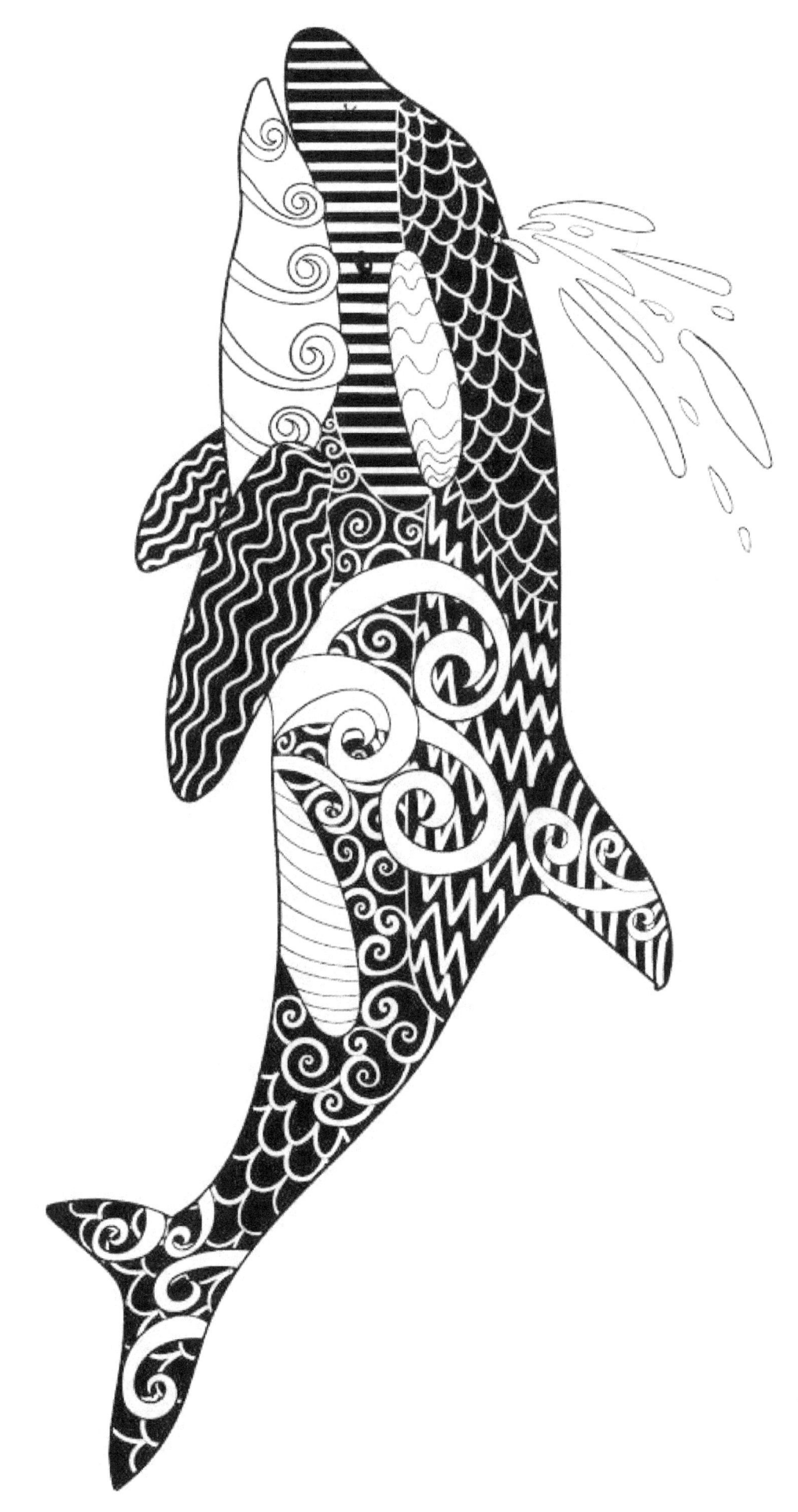

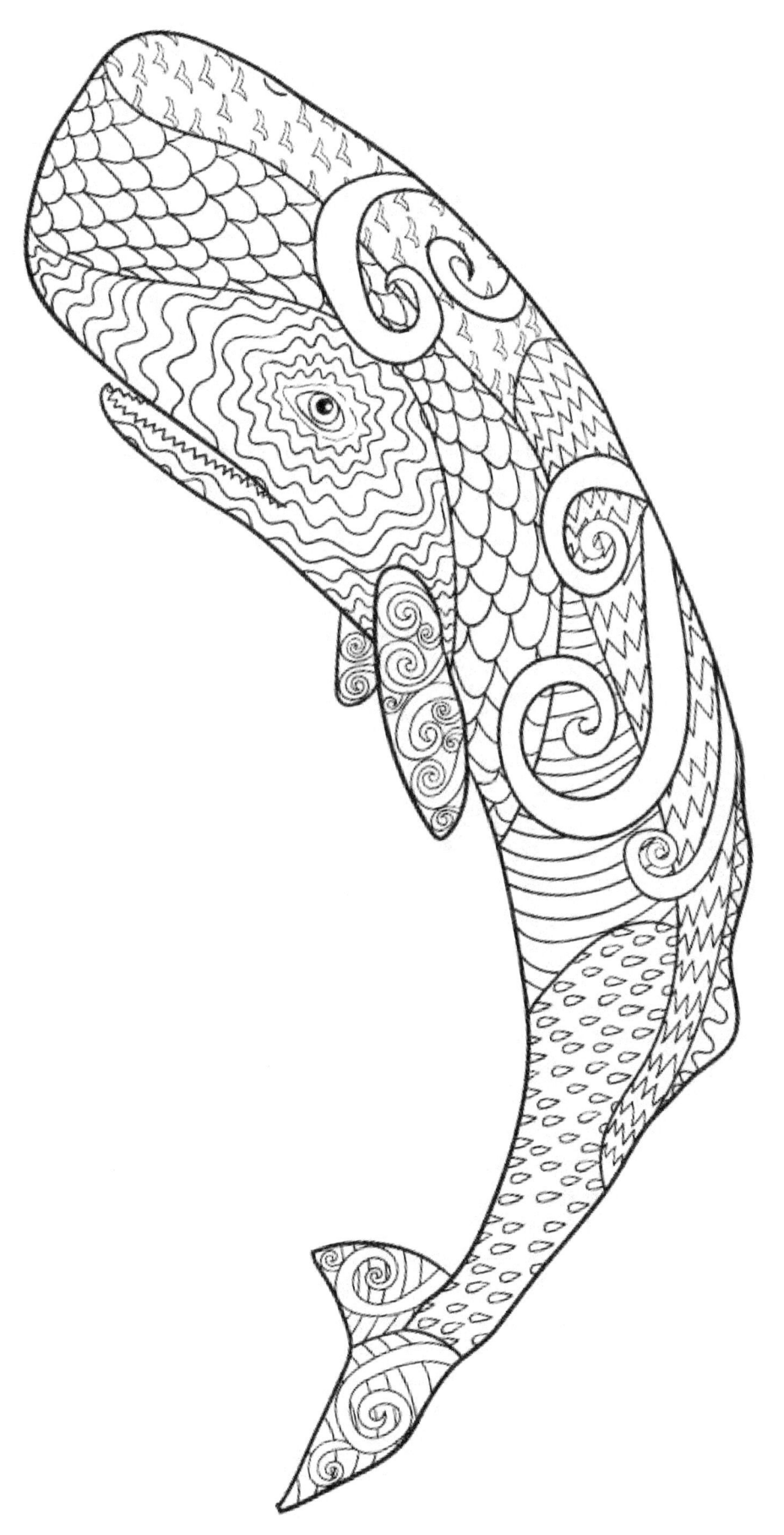

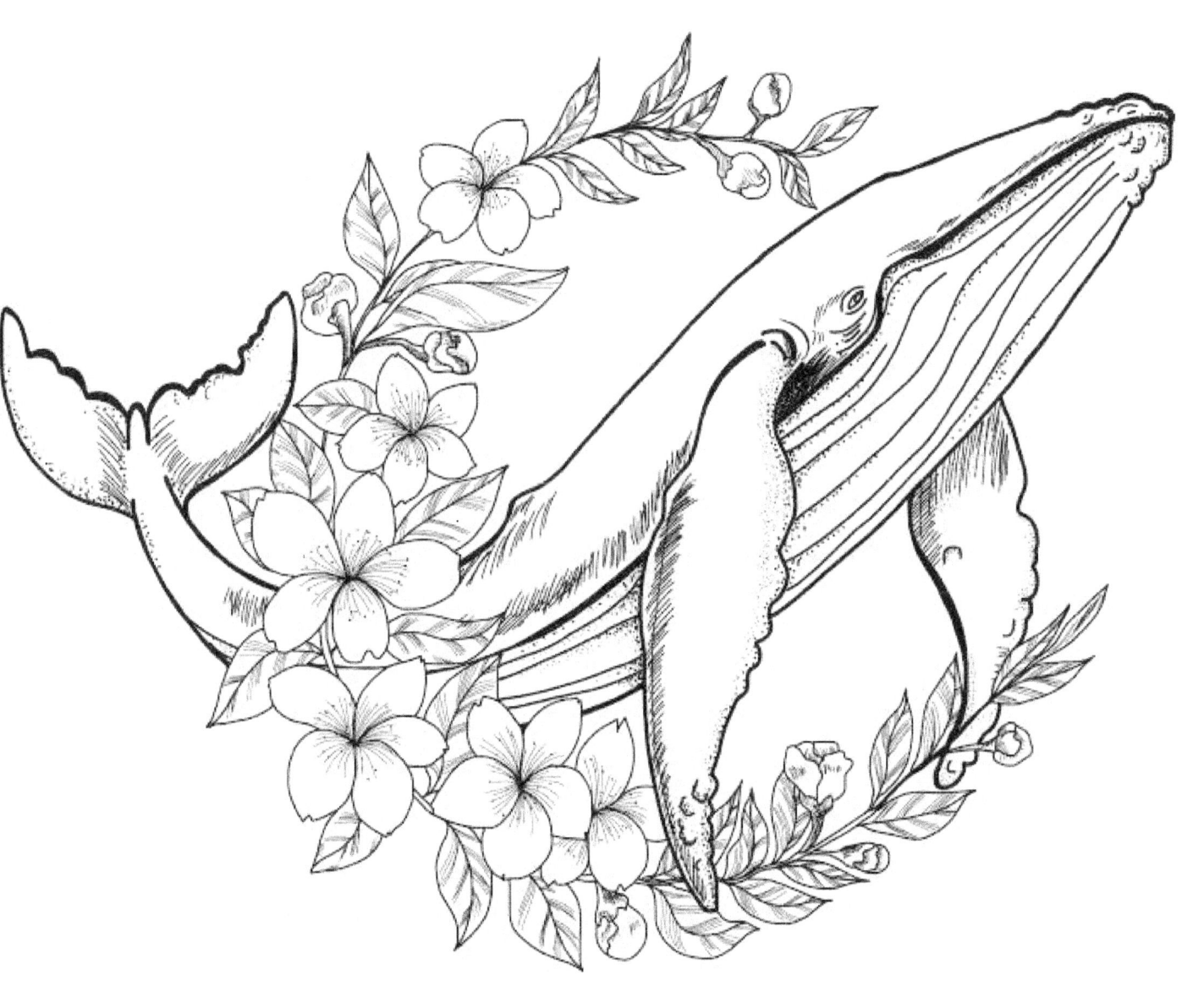

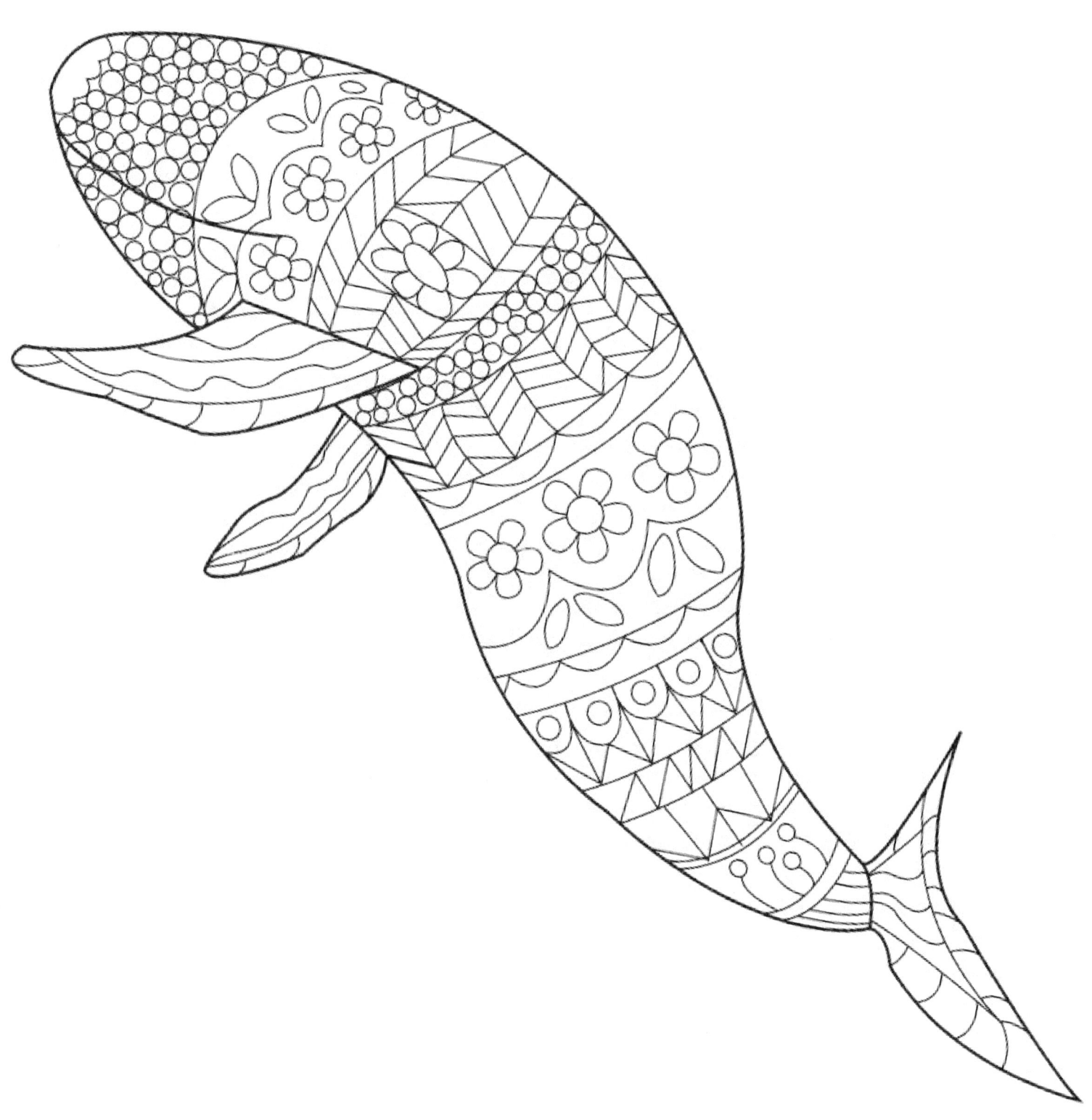

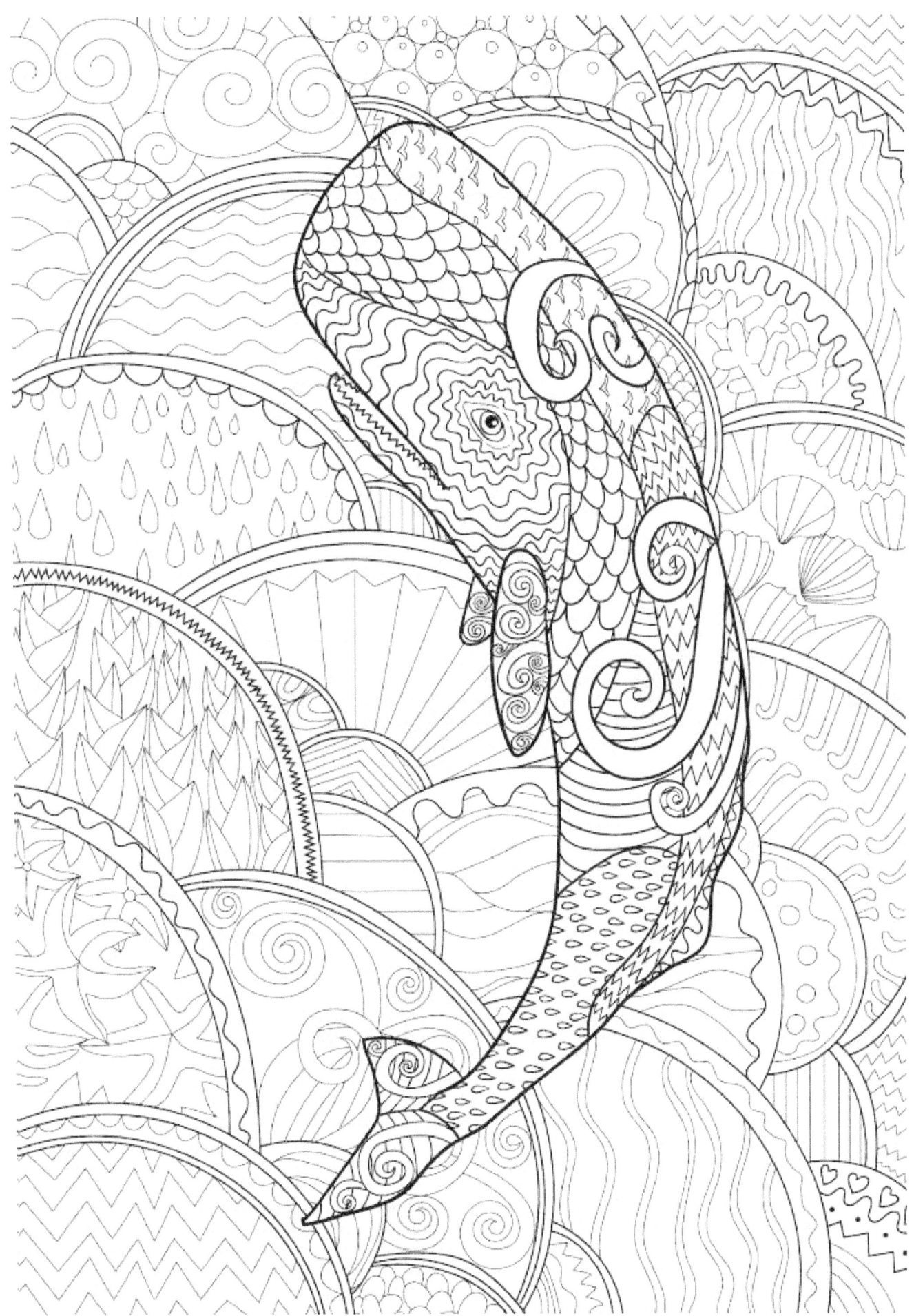

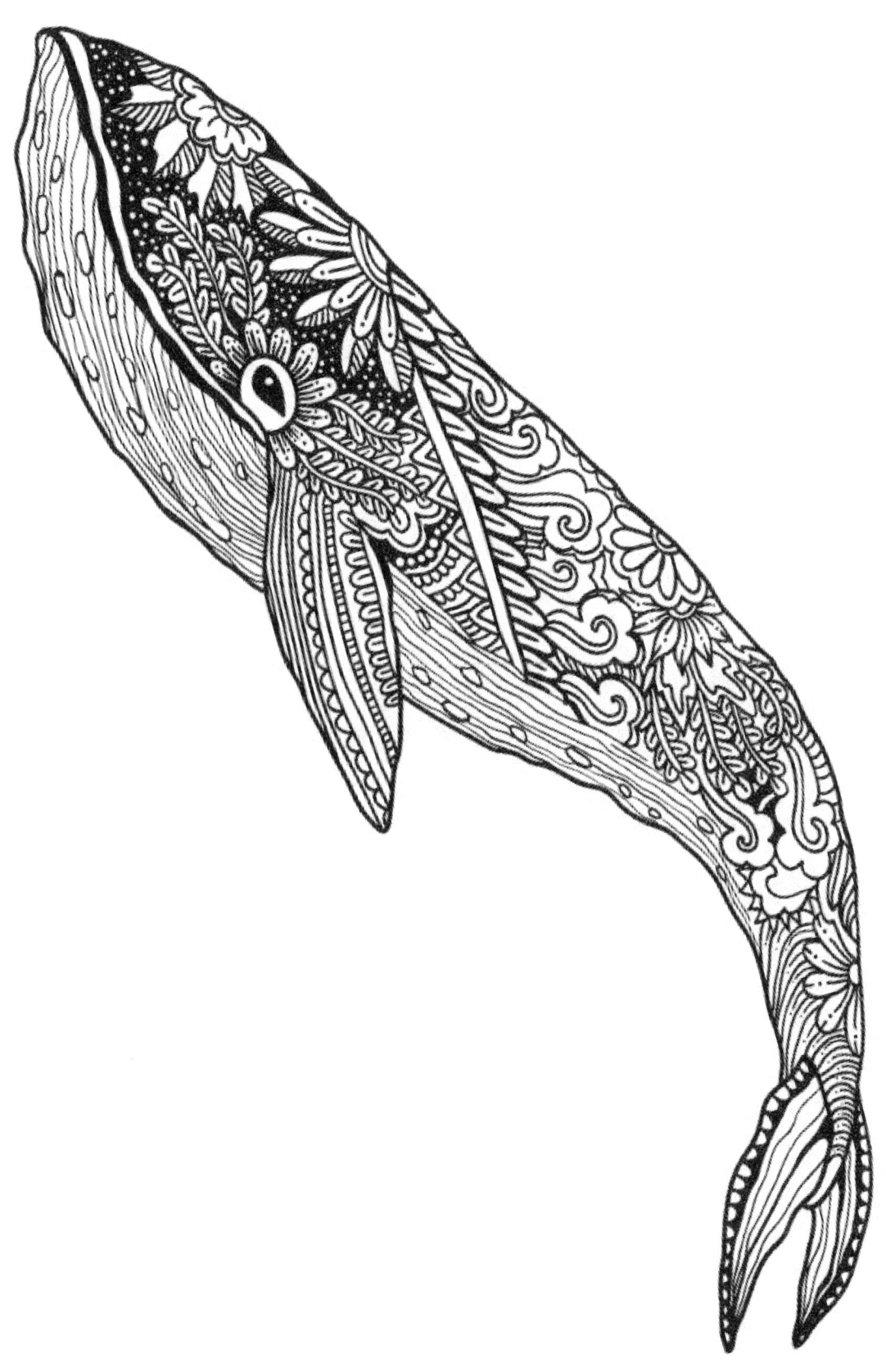

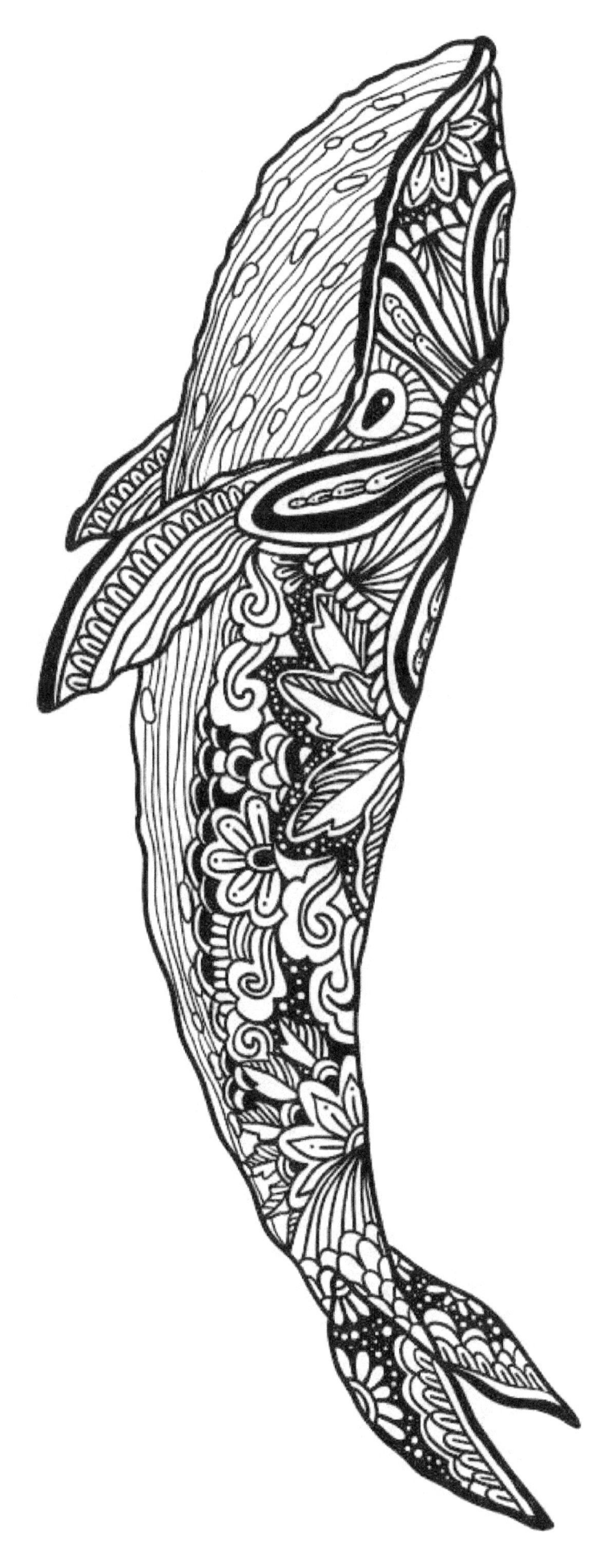

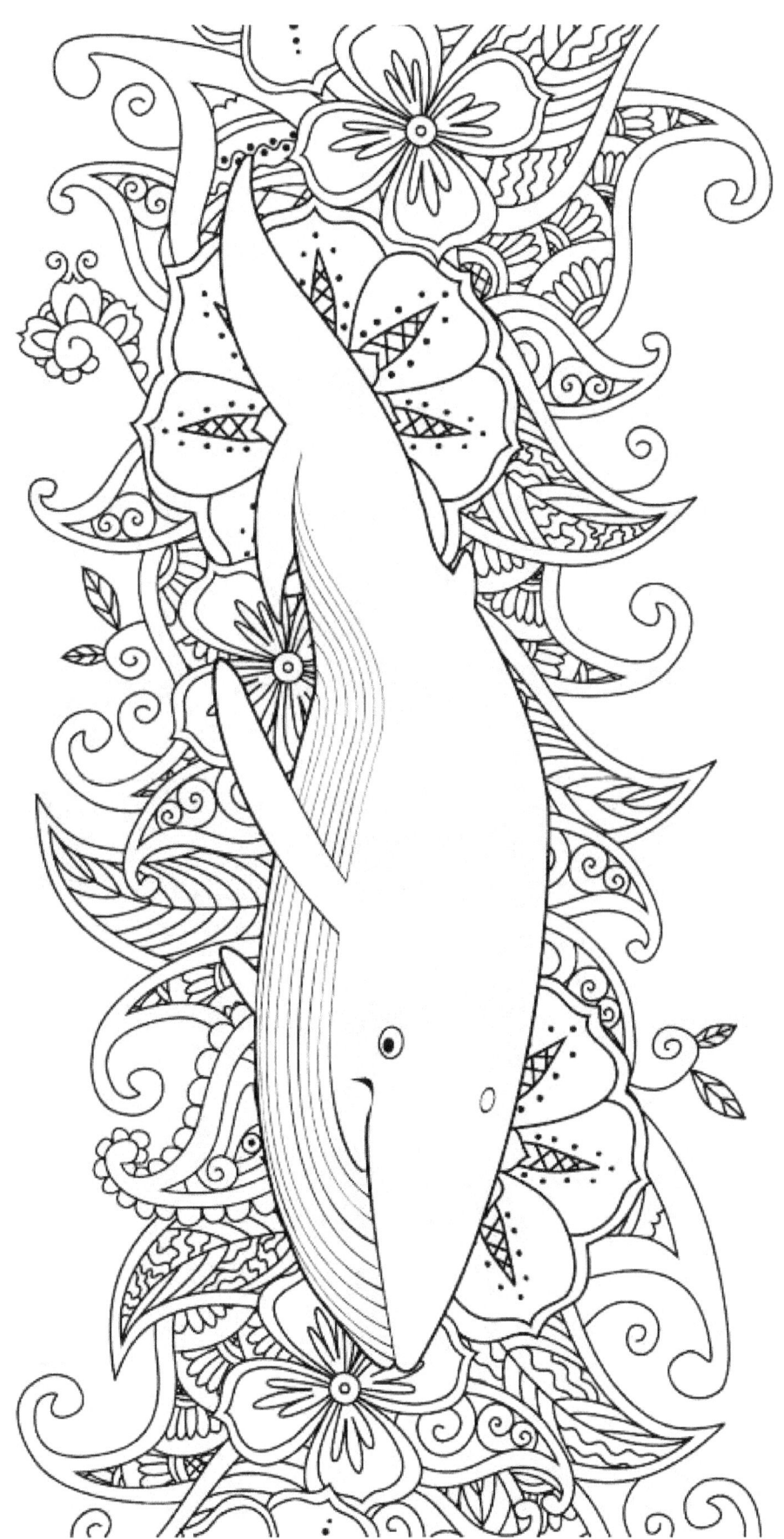

www.ingramcontent.com/pod-product-compliance
Lightning Source LLC
Chambersburg PA
CBHW081218170526
45165CB00009B/2862